LOCUSTS AT THE EDGE OF SUMMER

OTHER BOOKS BY JOHN BALABAN

Poetry

AFTER OUR WAR (University of Pittsburgh Press, 1974).
Lamont Prize
BLUE MOUNTAIN (Unicorn Press, 1982)
WORDS FOR MY DAUGHTER (Copper Canyon Press, 1991).
National Poetry Series

Translation

CA DAO VIETNAM: A BILINGUAL ANTHOLOGY OF VIETNAMESE
FOLK POETRY (Unicorn Press, 1974)

Nonfiction

VIETNAM: THE LAND WE NEVER KNEW (Chronicle Books, 1989)
REMEMBERING HEAVEN'S FACE (Simon & Schuster/Poseidon,
1991)

Fiction

THE HAWK'S TALE (Harcourt Brace Jovanovich, 1988)
COMING DOWN AGAIN (Simon & Schuster/Fireside, 1989)

JOHN BALABAN

Locusts at the Edge of Summer

NEW & SELECTED POEMS

 COPPER CANYON PRESS

Publication of this book is supported by a grant from the National Endowment for the Arts and a grant from the Lannan Foundation. Additional support to Copper Canyon Press has been provided by the Andrew W. Mellon Foundation, the Lila Wallace–Reader's Digest Fund, and the Washington State Arts Commission. Copper Canyon Press is in residence with Centrum at Fort Worden State Park.

ACKNOWLEDGMENTS: Some of these poems have appeared in *After Our War* (University of Pittsburgh, 1974), *The Alaska Quarterly Review, Asian Art and Culture, Blue Mountain* (Unicorn Press, 1982), *Witness*, and *Words for My Daughter* (Copper Canyon Press, 1991). Thanks to Janet Huston for her assistance with *Skagit Landscape, 1982.*

Library of Congress Cataloging-in-Publication Data
Balaban, John 1943–
Locusts at the Edge of Summer: NEW AND SELECTED POEMS / by John Balaban
p. cm.
ISBN 1-55659-123-3
I. Title.
PS3552.A44L63 1997
811'.54 – DC21   97-4654

COPPER CANYON PRESS
P.O. BOX 271, PORT TOWNSEND, WASHINGTON 98368

CONTENTS

99 *Part Three: Viewing the New World Order*

PART ONE

Speak, Memory

The proper subjects for poetry are love, virtue, and war.
   – *Dante,* DE VULGARI ELOQUENTIA, *Book II*

It's impossible to forget Vietnam, even if memories are obsolete.
   – *John Steinbeck, IV, "The Coconut Monk,"* LOKA 2

SPEAK, MEMORY

1 The Book and the Lacquered Box

So the Soul, that Drop, that Ray
Of the clear Fountain of Eternal Day,
Could it within the humane flow'r be seen.
  — Andrew Marvell, "On a Drop of Dew"

The ink-specked sheets feel like cigar leaf;
its crackling spine flutters up a mildewed must.
Unlike the lacquered box which dry-warp detonated
– shattering pearled poet, moon, and willow pond –
the book survived to beg us both go back
to the Bibliothèque in the Musée at the Jardin in Saigon,
where I would lean from ledges of high windows
to see the zoo's pond, isled with Chinese pavilion,
arched bridge where kids fed popcorn to gulping carp,
and shaded benches, where whores fanned their make-up,
at ease because a man who feeds the peacocks
can't be that much of a beast. A boat ride,
a soda, a stroll through the flower beds.
On weekends the crowds could forget the war.
At night police tortured men in the bear pits,
one night a man held out the bag of his own guts,
which streamed and weighed in his open hands,
and offered them to a bear. Nearby, that night,
the moon was caught in willows by the pond,
shone scattered in droplets on the flat lotus pads,
each bead bright like the dew in Marvell's rose.

A cool ceramic block, a brick
just larger than one's cheek,
cream-colored, bordered in blue,
a finely cracked glaze, but smooth,
a hollow bolster on which one lays
his face before it disappears
in curls of acrid opium fumes
slowly turning in the tropical room
lit by a lampwick's resinous light
which flickers on the floor and throws
shadows snaking up a wall.
The man who serves us with his pipes,
with nicotined and practiced hands,
works a heated wad of rosin
"cooked the color of a cockroach wing"
into the pinprick of the fat pipebowl.
He says, "Draw." One long draw
that pulls in combers of smoke rolling
down the lungs like the South China Sea,
crashing on the mind's frail shell
that rattles, then wallows and fills with sand.

I woke on wobbly legs to human cries.
Next door were Flynn and Stone
shouting and beating up an older man
they collared trying to steal their bikes.
Stone banged an M-16 against the fellow's ear
then struck him in the stomach with its butt.
He doubled up and wheezed for air;
they slammed him out and down the stairs
and, red and sweating, walked back in.
I stammered "no" but much too late;

my words were lifting up like bubbles
rocking off the ocean's floor.
Ten days later, they were dead. Flynn
and Stone, who dealt in clarities of force,
who motorcycled out to report war,
shot down together. Dead on Highway One.
Some twenty years ago. Their only headrest
this pillow of dreams and calmest sleep
which once held echoes like a shell
now sits upon my study shelf
and ebbs out muffled echoes like a bell.

3 Prince Buu Hoi's Watch

A long story. Of love and perfidy
ticking away in an old Omega
with a cracked crystal and a dusty face,
which the Prince's English friend gave me
just after his heart attack and early death.
We sat in her home in the Villa Segur.
"It's awful having it here," she said.
Above the mantle from which she took the watch
was her photograph from years before
in sundress and shady hat, in Saigon,
with the Prince and Diem and Henry Cabot Lodge,
all cordial in their tropical white suits.
Lodge was smiling with tall, paternal grace
at the pudgy little man, earnest with good will,
whom we liked to call "the Churchill of Asia."
Diem would die the next day. Lodge already knew.
And Patricia and Prince Buu Hoi, Minister of Health
and nearly the fixer of a separate peace, would flee
with sympathies from the French Ambassador.
One listens to the watch and sunlight shifts

as shadows shake through threshing palms,
through banyan and great sprays of bougainvillea.
The time that it keeps best is past.

4 The Perfume Vial

Its smooth shape fits easily in the palm
as one takes it from the shelf to see
the little mandarin with outstretched arms,
cap, queue, and courtly gown.
One simple question strikes me as I look:
The doves which flutter just above his hands
– are they flying to or from them?

LO, HE SEES FOUR MEN LOOSE, WALKING IN THE MIDST OF THE FIRE

Christians have always been pilgriming;
setting out with clamshell hat and clapper;
begging barefoot and beating their backs.
Hard-seeking fellows, scabbing their skins;
swigging down wormwood, gulping down gall.
Just as soon would they fry on pyres
of martyrdom as bathe in a river of mercy.
Yet, ever since pitch-dipped Christians
lighted Nero's dinner parties, we have
understood the purgation of fire. Fire
shall come to roast up Babylon; fire shall
teach Ezekiel; fire shall light Job's pain.
Nowhere but in the bible of the spirit
could Shadrach, Meshach, and Abednego
crack jokes in Nebuchadnezzar's fiery furnace.
O Lord, I go into a land where napalm
makes men dance a crazy jig; where
Nero sets his sights by human flares.
I ask for clear water, good earth, and air.

AUTUMN LANDSCAPE

Drop by drop rain slaps the banana leaves.
Praise whoever's skill sketched this desolate scene:
the lush, dark canopies of the gnarled trees;
the long river, sliding smooth and white.
Tilting my wine flask, I am drunk with rivers and hills.
My bag, filled with wind and moonlight, weighs on my back,
sags with poems. Look, and love even men.
Whoever sees this landscape is stunned.

from the Vietnamese of Ho Xuan Huong

ALONG THE MEKONG

1 Crossing on the Mekong Ferry,
Reading the August 14 *New Yorker*

Near mud-tide mangrove swamps, under the drilling sun,
the glossy cover, styled green print, struck the eye:
trumpet-burst yellow blossoms, grapevine leaves,
– nasturtiums or pumpkin flowers? They twined
in tangles by our cottage in Pennsylvania.
Inside, another article by Thomas Whiteside.
2, 4, 5-T, teratogenicity in births;
South Vietnam ⅐th defoliated; residue
in rivers, foods, and mothers' milk.
With a scientific turn of mind I can understand
that malformations in lab mice may not occur in children
but when, last week, I ushered hare-lipped, tusk-toothed kids
to surgery in Saigon, I wondered, what did they drink
that I have drunk? What dioxin, picloram, arsenic
have knitted in my cells, in my wife now carrying
our first child. Pigs were squealing in a truck.
Through the slats, I saw one lather the foam in its mouth.

2 River Market

Under the tattered umbrellas, piles of live eels
sliding in flat tin pans. Catfish flip for air.
Sunfish, gutted and gilled, cheek plates snipped.
Baskets of ginger roots, ginseng, and garlic cloves;
pails of shallots, chives, green citrons. Rice grain
in pyramids. Pig halves knotted with mushy fat.
Beef haunches hung from fist-size hooks. Sorcerers,
palmists, and, under a tarp: thick incense, candles.
Why, a reporter, or a cook, could write this poem

if he had learned dictation. But what if I said,
simply suggested, that all this blood fleck,
muscle rot, earth root and earth leaf, scraps
of glittery scales, fine white grains, fast talk,
gut grime, crab claws, bright light, sweetest smells
– Said: a human self; a mirror held up before.

3 Waiting for a Boat to Cross Back

Slouched on a bench under some shade,
I overhear that two men shot each other on the street,
and I watch turkey cocks drag cornstalk fans
like mad, rivaling kings in kabuki
sweeping huge sleeve and brocaded train.
The drab hens huddle, beak to beak,
in queenly boredom of rhetoric and murder.
A mottled cur with a grease-paint grin
laps up fish scales and red, saw-toothed gills
gutted from panfish at the river's edge.

THE GUARD AT THE BINH THUY BRIDGE

How still he stands as mists begin to move,
as curling, morning billows creep across
his cooplike, concrete sentry perched mid-bridge
over mid-muddy river. Stares at bush green banks
which bristle rifles, mortars, men – perhaps.
No convoys shake the timbers. No sound
but water slapping boat sides, bank sides, pilings.
He's slung his carbine barrel down to keep
the boring dry, and two banana-clips instead of one
are taped to make, now, forty rounds instead
of twenty. Droplets bead from stock to sight;
they bulb, then strike his boot. He scrapes his heel,
and sees no box bombs floating toward his bridge.
Anchored in red morning mist a narrow junk
rocks its weight. A woman kneels on deck
staring at lapping water. Wets her face.
Idly the thick Rach Binh Thuy slides by.
He aims. At her. Then drops his aim. Idly.

MAU THAN

A Poem at Tet for To Lai Chanh

1 Friend, the Old Man that was last year
   has had his teeth kicked in; in tears
   he spat back blood and bone, and died.
   Pielike, the moon has carved the skies
   a year's worth to the eve. It is Tet
   as I sit musing at your doorstep,
   as the yellowed leaves scratch and clutter.
   The garden you dug and plotted
   before they drafted you, is now
   stony, dry, and wanting a trowel.
   "For my wife," you said, taking a plum,
   but the day never came nor will it come
   to bring your bride from Saigon.
   Still the boats fetch stone, painted eyes on
   their prows, plowing the banana-green river;
   and neighbor children splash and shiver
   where junks wait to unload their rock.
   But shutters locked, the door of your house is locked.

2 A year it was of barbarities
   each heaped on the other like stones
   on a man stoned to death.
   One counts the ears on the GI's belt.
   Market meats come wrapped in wrappers
   displaying Viet Cong disemboweled.
   Cries come scattering like shot.
   You heard them and I heard them.
   The night you left I turned off Hoa Binh
   and saw a mined jeep, the charred family.
   A Vietnamese cop minded the wreckage:

his gold buckteeth were shining
in a smile like a bright brass whistle.
Can you tell me how the Americans,
officers and men, on the night of
the mortaring, in the retching hospital,
could snap flash photos of the girl whose
vagina was gouged out by mortar fragments?
One day we followed in a cortege
of mourners, among the mourners, slowing walking,
hearing the clop of the monk's knocking stick.

3 If there were peace, this river would be
a peaceful place. Here at your door
thoughts arrive like rainwater, dotting,
overspreading a dry, porous rock.
In a feathery drizzle, a man and wife
are fishing the river. The sidling waves
slap at her oar as she ladles the water
and steadies the boat with bored precision.
His taut wrists fling whirring weights;
the flying net swallows a circle of fish.
His ear wears a raindrop like a jewel.
Here at evening one might be as quiet
as the rain blowing faintly off
the eaves of a rice boat sliding home.
Coming to this evening
after a rain, I found a buff bird
perched in the silvery-green branches
of a water-shedding spruce. It was
perched like a peaceful thought. Then
I thought of the Book of Luke and, indeed,
of the nobleman who began a sojourn
to find a kingdom and return.

4 Out of the night, wounded
 with the gibberings of dogs,
 wheezing with the squeaks of rats,
 out of the night, its belly split
 by jet whine and mortar blast,
 scissored by the claws of children,
 street sleepers, ripping their way free
 from cocoons of mosquito netting
 to flee the rupturing bursts
 and the air dancing with razors
 – out, I came, to safe haven.
 Nor looked, nor asked further.
 Who would? What more? I said.
 I said: Feed and bathe me.
 In Japan I climbed Mt. Hiei in midwinter.
 The deer snuffled my mittens.
 The monkeys came to beg.
 I met Moses meeting God in the clouds.
 The cold wind cleared my soul.
 The mountain was hidden in mist. Friend,
 I am back to gather the blood in a cup.

CARCANET: AFTER OUR WAR

For thy Carcanets of Pearle, shalt thou have Carcanets of Spyders,
or the Greene Venomous Flye, Cantharides.
  — *Thomas Nashe,* CHRISTE'S TEARES OVER JERUSALEM

When we blighted the fields, the harvests replied:
"You have blighted your flesh." Muck-marrowed,
bones ungluing like book paste; nerve hems
shredded or grimed in something foul, leaking,
we visit each other like a plague. Kiss-Kiss.
Intelligence is helplessly evil; words lie.
Morally quits, Hieronymo gnashes off his tongue,
spits out the liver-lump to a front-row lap,
but wishes, then to explain; even: to recite poetry.
Yesterday a pig snouting for truffles uncovered
moles, blind and bellyful of *Paradise Lost.*
Gleeful, let us go somewhere to curse God and die.

To market they came from land and sea, the air:
"A mighty fine place," one General agreed.
They reined in their horses and looked down to find
an old beggar woman sneaking by in their shadows.
"Call in the Doctor," barked the Seal from the Sea.
A Fourth Horseman reined up, brandishing a smile
for half the lady's face was a red hanging bag,
one eye a wart-strudel, her chin a grainy sac.
She begged. The Doctor-General proffered a pin,
"My Lady, in our hour of need." He pick-pricked a node.
A yellow milk-water splashed her blouse, spurted
curdles on the Horsemen's boots, streaked to the gutter,
filled up the streets and gushed against doorsills.
The old lady cackled; the four generals beamed,
and summoned a palfrey for Their Lady to ride.

They had found Home, were Active. As they rode off
the hooves of their horses spattered the walks.

At that the fat bullets started to jump;
some whined to splice the prism of an eye, others
bled the marrow from a rib. Windshields spidered;
the Spiders ran off, eight-legged, fast, with money,
more than you can guess, stuck to the hairy legs.
Spontaneous Generation: the Bore-Flies sang,
"Every wound has two lips, so give us a kiss."
Then a two-headed cow jumped over the moon,
kicked over its lantern. Fire caught Straw.
The cow burst like a 500-lb. bomb. Everyone
came running – all the old folks – Slit Eye
and Spilled Guts, Fried Face and little Missy Stumps.
They plaited a daisy chain. This necklace. For you.

THE SHIP OF REDEMPTION

The bell of Linh Mu pagoda tolls,
awakening our drowsy souls,
probing, reminding us of debts,
washing us clean of worldly dust.
A boat crosses to the Buddha Lands.

a folk poem from Hue

THE GARDENIA IN THE MOON

for David Lane Gitelson, 1942–1968

1 In Pennsylvania Woods

The wind was husking, hushing, hosting,
worrying the slimed leaves of the wood.
Moon's light, thick as Witches' Butter,
stuck to branch bark and to lifting leaves.
Standing under fitful oaks, under Orion
bullying the gods, I saw car lights
stabbing past the rain-blacked trunks,
and heard peacocks shriek, an owl,
hoot. Men had landed on the moon.
As men shot dirty films in dirty motel rooms,
guerrillas sucked cold rice and fish.
Wind-spooked leaves scratched my cheek.
Blood on the bark stung my hand.
In a puddle's moon eye I saw a shape:
A machine gun was cracking like slapping sticks.
A yelling man smacked into the smooth canal.

2 MONTHLY REPORT — AGRICULTURE
DATE: October, 1967
STATION: Hue-Duc, An-Giang – Region IV
IVS TEAM MEMBER: Dave Gitelson

At least two varieties of fruit trees here suffer badly from disease.
Infected custard apple trees, "mang cau ta," produce fruit that's
hard, black and spore-filled. This is a very prevalent disease, so
much so that people are discouraged from planting this tree, for-
merly a popular orchard variety. Another disease affects jackfruit

trees, "mit," the fruit first develops brown patches then turns mushy. I'd appreciate advice on how to deal with these diseases. Dithane and other fungicides are available in Long Xuyen but they're expensive.

Previously I've had talks with the province and MSCR on possible ways to reduce civilian war casualties, e.g. get the families of soldiers out of the remote outposts by providing them housing in more secure areas. Late last month, after one man was killed and another wounded by air-fire in a free fire zone west of Vong-The Village, the local people made some suggestions that might also apply to other areas. First they asked the zone be suspended, but in lieu of that they said that if the outposts closest to the zone, which in this case includes a company headquarters, could have been contacted by radio, the men might not have been shot, since they were known to several of the local soldiers.

3 A Cyclo Ride to Town

Early evening air cools the cheek;
the dust is down on the rutted road.
Lurching handlebars as we wheel up,
the cyclo driver hoots and jings his bell
at the dog that lolls panting in our way.
The weary bitch drags off her heavy tits.

From the bouncing carriage, one studies
the old man's dry calves, bulging out
blue ropy veins as tendons stretch and ease.
An axle, a fender, his head bobbles
on a rooster's neck. Teeth gritting dust,
he pedals us past a tin bus decaying
by the roadside: bleached, roofless,
floorboards dropped, the stripped seat-frames
jut like knobby vertebrae upon a beach.

We pass the pond-links where fishermen,
anonymous as jellyfish tracing a shore,
hurl parabolas to snag the glinting carp,
And hopping home from market, a one-legged girl
pauses to tuck a pant leg to her stump.

Jolting past a dust-caked banana grove,
by the Post Gate we come upon the crowd
gawking at the farmer hauled in like a pig:
riddled dead, blood-splotched, trussed to a pole.
Striking the smooth macadam of a city street,
we roll down the boulevard, past the market
along the river sliding under reeling birds,
past the dry fountain with its sandbagged gun nest
and stop at the French governor's empty mansion,
roofed with orange tiles, walled with chipping stucco.
The gate guard salutes, then grins with history
as an American strides the pebbled walkway
to the garden at the rear of the elegant house,
whose formal paths, boxwoods, flower beds
– laid in a helplessly exact geometry –
have been tank-tracked by the armored unit
bivouacked beneath the high, threshing palms.

The scent of gardenia and campsmoke shifts
through the strung laundries and poncho tents.

4 MONTHLY REPORT – AGRICULTURE
PERIOD: December, 1967
STATION: Hue-Duc, An-Giang – Region IV
IVS TEAM MEMBER: Dave Gitelson

3 weeks ago Tuesday morning there was an airstrike on the outskirts of Tan Tay Hamlet, Vong-The Village, which killed immediately 4 children 2 women and 3 men and wounded 12 others. In

two families both parents were killed. Later one of the wounded, a man, died. A community of 33 families was wiped off the map. Their homes were mostly destroyed along with their boats and livestock. The survivors arrived in the market with nothing but the clothes they were wearing at the time of the attack, that is with no bedding or food. I've been told this was an unavoidable accident, the victims were at fault; and all necessary precautions were taken. I'm not satisfied that this is true. I have the following facts and questions in mind:

1) The Vietnamese and American military were jointly responsible for the strike. The planes that did the bombing were Vietnamese Air Force. There was an L-19 in the area with a Vietnamese observer and an American pilot-observer. The District and Province gave their approval. Their MACV counterparts say they're just advisors – but none of them advised against the attack.

MACV claims there were VC in the area dug in and firing at the planes. All right, the L-19 was up and he ought to know. But no VC casualties came my way. And it's hard to have total faith in MACV Intelligence when 24 hours after the attack there were people at MACV subsector who didn't know the majority of casualties were women and children and 3 weeks after the attack a senior officer at MACV Long-Xuyen apparently wasn't certain any children had been killed at all. But what if the area had been swarming with VC. L-19 pilots in Region I have told me they'd never advise a strike if there were civilians in the area. There haven't been any American casualties in Hue-Duc that I know of since I've been here; the pressure doesn't exist like near DaNang and Hue. Why should an airstrike have been called with civilians so close? If those had been American kids on the ground, could such a thing possibly have happened?

5 Gardenia

The scent of gardenia and campsmoke shifts
across laundries, hammocks, and tents.
With white, thick, waxy, double petals a jasmine
gardenia reeks, a prostitute in the stripped garden.
Under a planked jetty, soldiers and their little sons
skinny-dip, foaming the silted river with suds.
Below a lotus blooming in the mucky shallows,
a crab sidles through a basket rotting in the mud.
Midstream, huge egrets lift off bamboo isles.
I hear my name called: "Mr. American!"
by a pajamaed young mother who grins and beckons,
slapping a broken slipper and waddling my way.
Closing to her thumb the fingers of a white hand,
in the bud-hole of those loose doubled petals
she pokes her other index, and smiles. Tilting her chin,
she pokes her finger again and again and smiles.

6 I.V.S. Memorandum
TO: Dan Whitfield   DATE: Jan. 30,1968
FROM: Roger Montgomery
SUBJECT: A Chronology

On Friday evening, Jan. 26, I met the plane coming in from Long
Xuyen, bringing Tom Fox, who was to change planes and go on to
Saigon, after visiting Phil Yang in Long Xuyen. Tom brought the
first word that Dave had been captured and reported killed. After
hearing all of the information that Tom had, I quickly returned to
the CORDS office to call you and relay the small amount of info that
we had. That evening I called Col. Lane in Long Xuyen, and also
Bob Flores called me in Can Tho. The first reports were that a
man who had been called a "taxi driver" (perhaps of a water taxi
boat?) had reported to officials in Hue Duc district that he had
seen Dave captured by four VC and taken off a distance into a

woodsy section and then heard four shots. That evening there was also a report that somebody in Hue Duc had seen a body. It was not confirmed by any American or Vietnamese Government official that it was Dave and there was no certainty where it was. The next morning I drove to Long Xuyen with John Balaban....

Col. Lane, who in his briefing to John and me expressed his dislike for Dave and related how they had had serious disagreements (especially concerning the bombing incident reported in Dave's last monthly report), said that they were making all efforts to recover his body but that he had been consulting his rule books all morning to find out if the military should handle civilians bodies, and couldn't find a guiding ruling....

...[Dave] also was onto something that was extremely sensitive, which he had mentioned to Tom Fox and me just the previous Wednesday (or Thursday) that one day prior to Senator Edward Kennedy's trip to Hue Duc district to visit the refugees that the refugee chief had come out and told the refugees that if they spoke out complaining to Senator Kennedy about treatment in the refugee camp that he would have them killed or imprisoned or such.

7 A Garden Becomes a Moon

Think of hot mercury trickling out
or molten silver pouring in a dish.
The webs and sluggish river-loops
winked up the sun's burst blooms
as the plane droned home to Saigon.
Zipped in a green vinyl sack
shutting the stinks together, the body
shook on the rivet-rattling floor.
Strapped in, the two friends sat
staring at each other's shoes, the sack,
their hands, the banana-green sack. The pilot

sipped warm Coke and radioed the morgue.
In the cratered Strike Zone far below
smoke drifted up from a fragmented tomb.
A man burnt incense at his father's grave.

Before their clouding, before closing, one sees
oneself in the eyes of the dead,
eyes of the children cut down like skinny chickens,
eyes of the small-breasted women, wiry men.
Those who became completely wise cried out
as the slugs shattered the windshield,
glass flying into spider webs,
as skipping bullets slivered their eyes.
Gitelson, do-gooder? a fool?
Am I some Christer or your corpse-monger?
Dead, I am your father, brother. Dead, we are your son.

THE WATER BUFFALO
HANOI, 1972

The rain drizzled and shifted
over rippling green fields of rice.
Every drop will grow a grain.

The lop-eared banana leaves
opened an umbrella over me
and I sank into an ancient hush.

An old man with a buffalo
stood at the end of the path.
Both were carved in wood.

Without a word the old man
parted a curtain of leaves
to let me into his house.

I stepped across the threshold
and froze before a gaping hole,
a crater bigger than a grave.

Smoke rose from ashes,
black smoke curling in the wind.
Dry wells, instead of walls.

My host slid down to the bottom,
calling me, with beckoning hand,
to his family in the pit.

His grandson – a tuft of hair,
His old woman – the handle of a pot,
His strapping sons – bloody stones.

His pretty girls – threads of cloth,
His sons-in-law – sandal thongs,
His daughters-in-law – lumps of earth.

His brother, on a visit – a broken stool,
His great-grandson, still in the womb
of his mother – a banana shoot.

The shoot, as if still growing,
had a green bud which resembled
the clenched fist of a baby.

...To have lived a long life honestly,
to have raised a big family
by yourself, and in your old age

to be left alone with your buffalo,
the only living creature
with whom to share your sorrow...

The inventions of America, those
gadgets, machines, technical wonders –
is this what they are for?

*translated from the Bulgarian (with
Elena Christova) of Blaga Dimitrova*

PALINDROME FOR CLYDE COREIL IN SAIGON

Pigeons flutter in the eaves of the Music Bldg;
here there are a number of beautiful women.
Amid the clutter of books on my desk,
I prop my feet, lean back, and read.
Hot lunches are served at a cafeteria nearby.
Each afternoon, I pick up *The Times*.
A secretary brews coffee. I get paid for talking
to students who don't care what I say
about subjects I don't care to talk about.
When I can afford them, I buy good cigars.

Every now and then, you get cigars from home.
Puffing on one, you dicker with a shopgirl
over the price of a breakfast of French bread
and black coffee in a sugar-bottomed glass.
You study newsprint on a wrapper of dried squid.
Elephant grass and rice fields expand beyond the city.
Returning at evening, your feet plod along a street
crunching with fishheads, roaches, and shattered glass.
A bargirl telephones to see if you'll be in. Outside,
music flutters in the wings of rising pigeons.

NEWS UPDATE

for Erhart, Gitelson, Flynn and Stone, happily dead and gone.

Well, here I am in the *Centre Daily Times*
back-to-back with the page-one refugees
fleeing the crossfire, pirates, starvation.
Familiar faces. We followed them
through defoliated forests, cratered fields,
past the blasted water buffalo,
the shredded tree lines, the human head
dropped on the dusty road, eyes open,
the dusty road which called you all to death.

One skims the memory like a Moviola,
editing out the candid shots: Sean Flynn
dropping his camera and grabbing a gun
to muster the charge and retake the hill.
"That boy," the black corporal said,
"do in real life what his daddy do in movies."
Dana Stone, in an odd moment of mercy,
sneaking off from Green Beret assassins
to the boy they left for dead in the jungle.
Afraid of the pistol's report, Stone shut his eyes
and crushed the kid's throat with a bayonet.
Or, Erhart, sitting on his motorcycle
smiling and stoned in the Free Strike Zone
as he filmed the ammo explosion at Lai Khe.
It wasn't just a macho game. Marie-Laure de Decker
photographed the man aflame on the public lawn.
She wept and shook and cranked her Pentax
until a cop smashed it to the street. Then
there was the girl returned from captivity

with a steel comb fashioned from a melted-down tank,
or some such cliché, and engraved: "To Sandra
From the People's Fifth Battalion, Best Wishes."

Christ, most of them are long dead. Tim Page
wobbles around with a steel plate in his head.
Gitelson roamed the Delta in cut-away blue jeans
like a hippy Johnny Appleseed with a burlap sack
full of seeds and mimeographed tips for farmers
until we pulled him from the canal. His brains
leaked on my hands and knee. Or me, yours truly,
agape in the Burn Ward in Danang, a quonset hut,
a half a garbage can that smelled like Burger King,
listening to whimpers and nitrate fizzing on flesh
in a silence that simmered like a fly in a wound.

And here I am, ten years later,
written up in the local small-town press
for popping a loud-mouth punk in the choppers.
Oh, big sighs. Windy sighs. And ghostly laughter.

ERHART

1 Standing in a soybean field,
  on a rocky scarp above the sea,
  the two of us, in dispossessed thirties,
  scan nude bathers on the shore below,
  as gulls, winged flesh all salt,
  might scour for shellfish.
  Angry and red on Erhart's belly
  the football stitch stings with sweat
  where they cut into his cancer.
  But look at him here today:
  climbing cliffs, getting his peek,
  dismayed only that the naked man below
  who sidles into a tide-cut cave
  lures not a girl, but another gay.
  As I watch him watch a girl in the surf,
  Erhart remarks that "birds have nests;
  foxes have their holes, but the Son of Man
  hath nowhere to lay his head."
  "Birds have nests," I add. "Men have ancestors."
  Erhart's father died manic and alone.
  A whore-child gave birth to Erhart
  at twenty-seven, in Asia, across the Pacific
  that glints on these bathers and defies our stare.

2 Outside Middlesex hospital
  the student unions queue,
  marching behind a rent-all truck
  from which a band plays "Hello Dolly."
  They want bigger scholarships.
  Inside Middlesex, a blonde moppet
  zaps Erhart with cobalts
  to make his cancer go away,
  those narsty nodes, that ugly clavicle
  blossoming into a Kali-flower.
  She says it will be all right:
  Never once has she died
  for all the patients she's radiated.
  Erhart is going to India to meet
  a wonderful Indian guru, leaving England
  to its henna-haired boys and big women.
  Outside, the Bobbies badger the crowd.
  Inside Erhart's insides
  his ionized cells are blue with rage
  like Tantric demons blue-faced with rage.

3 At night, by the Ganges, by a pyre guttering
  foul smoke and gaseous licks of flame —
  by a dog gnawing the ankle and foot
  of a woman cremated during the day —
  Erhart, hunched as if he had a chest cold,
  pisses on a flat rock and looks up at stars,
  at Berenice's Hair, at the Lost Pleiades,

at Orion about to hurl his spear of stars.
In L.A., a G.P. thought Erhart had an ulcer.
The surgery didn't work. After the vegetable
diet, the German carrot-juice treatment,
the yoga chants, the asanas, the "breaths of fire,"
after the sautéed-lemon-rind cure,
the acupuncturist, the Reichian masseuse,
after all the death-defying fucking in London
Erhart has come to see Sai Baba
who can materialize Swiss watches
and pillars of holy ash. (But can he kill the Big C?)
What else is left? Filipino psychic surgeons?
If one plays at dying, he doesn't die at all.
(In a closet in my farmhouse in Pennsylvania
Erhart's manuscripts fill his flight bag,
stories and articles, published and unpublished,
the film clips he shot on battlefields in Vietnam.)
The river tide washes the embers of the dead.
Erhart, diving and flying in a whirl of methadone
and realization, watches for star-nesting birds;
spies a man-bird: beaked, crimson-winged,
with a body of gold – Garuda,
who routed the gods, their wheel of blades
who severed the snake guard, spat back its poison,
whose wing-beat rush could stop the world.
Who spat back the poison. Who dwells in the sun.

Keep moving, friend, and don't look down.

LETTER FROM A BARGIRL

(found in a typewriter)

```
                    my dearest darling
              hi/  how are you
          ihop eeveything is abight with you,iam fine
 ꞁꞁ imi    i miss you veryꞁ m uch
          doꞁ yꞁꞁꞁꞁ  you miss me/
                fuck you
              iwant to fuck yꞁuꞁ


          i think about you all time
          you alays in myꞁꞁ heart

         makee love nꞁ
                make . love . not.. war ........

     fuck....you


                    Monique
```

JOHN STEINBECK, IV (1947–1991)

I used to dread his calls, which pulled me out of bed
for twenty years since Vietnam, his drunken talk,
his deep insistence growling through the phone,
his irritation with my sleep, my middle class retreat.
We had been so close we shared each other's dreams

in Saigon, later, London, stoned by memories
of war, of R&R with Mekong river monks
who offered puzzled welcomes to the pals he dubbed
"lysergic Buddhists," now come to Phoenix Island, where
he played a bamboo flute and spoke of certain priests

from a line of jungle prophets schooled in crazy song:
the Master of the Western Peace, the Monk Who Sells Potatoes,
who breathed the Strange Perfume from Precious Mountain, all
unlettered peasants who erased his father's fame.
He knew I knew the pain he carried with his name.

His last call came at Tet the year before he died.
From an East L.A. pagoda he conned to take him in.
Dead broke except for his expensive name, he complained
the monks kept scolding him for drinking, said he smelled.
What would the spirits say in their heavenly report?

Indeed, what will they say in heavenly reports?
He played a bamboo flute and spoke of Buddhist priests.
That some friends knew the pain he carried with his name.
He visits time to time and tries to stir their dreams
with opium and amulets and scents from Precious Mountain.

THOUGHTS BEFORE DAWN

for Mary Bui Thi Khuy, 1944–1969

The bare oaks rock, and snowcrust tumbles down.
The creaking eave woke me thinking of you
crushed by a truck thirteen years ago
when the drunk ARVN lost the wheel.

We brought to better care the nearly lost,
the boy burned by white phosphorus, chin
glued to his chest; the scalped girl;
the triple amputee from the road-mined bus;
the kid without a jaw; the one with no nose.
You never wept in front of them, but waited
until the gurney rolled them into surgery.
I guess that's what amazed me most.
Why didn't you fall apart or quit?

Once, we flew two patched kids home,
getting in by Army chopper,
a Huey Black Cat that skimmed the sea.
When the gunner opened up on a whale
you closed your eyes and covered your ears
and your small body shook in your silk *ao dai.*

Oh, Mary. In this arctic night, I lie in my bed
and rehearse your smile, bright white teeth,
the funny way you rode your Honda 50: perched
so straight, silky hair bunned up in a brim hat,
front brim blown back, and dark glasses.
Brave woman, I hope you never saw the truck.

ON READING THE ANTHOLOGY OF THE TEN THOUSAND POETS

The ancients loved those poems with natural feel:
Clouds, wind, moon, snow. Flowers, rivers, crags.
A poem should contain strong tempered steel:
Today the poet must learn to lead a charge.

Ho Chi Minh

FOR MRS. CAM, WHOSE NAME MEANS "PRINTED SILK"

The ancients loved those poems with natural feel.
  – Ho Chi Minh, "On Reading the Ten Thousand Poets"

In Vietnam, poets brushed on printed silk
those poems about clouds, mountains, and love.
But now their poems are cased in steel.

You lived beyond the Pass of Clouds
along the Perfume River, in Hue,
whose name means "lily."

The war has blown away your past.
No poem can call it back.
How does one start over?

You raise your kids in southern California;
run a key punch from 9:00 to 5:00,
and walk the beach each evening,

marveling at curls broken bare in crushed shells,
at the sheen and cracks of laved, salted wood,
at the pearling blues of rock-stuck mussels

all broken, all beautiful, accidents
which remind you of your life, lost friends
and pieces of poems which made you whole.

In tidal pools, the pipers wade
on twiggy legs, stabbing for starfish
with scissoring, poking, needle bills.

The wide Pacific flares in sunset.
Somewhere over there was once your home.
You study the things which start from scratch.

Nicely like a pearl is a poem
begun with an accidental speck
from the ocean of the actual.

A grain, a grit, which once admitted
irritates the mantle of thought
and coats itself in lacquers of the mind.

AFTER OUR WAR

After our war, the dismembered bits
– all those pierced eyes, ear slivers, jaw splinters,
gouged lips, odd tibias, skin flaps, and toes –
came squinting, wobbling, jabbering back.
The genitals, of course, were the most bizarre,
inching along roads like glowworms and slugs.
The living wanted them back but good as new.
The dead, of course, had no use for them.
And the ghosts, the tens of thousands of abandoned souls
who had appeared like swamp fog in the city streets,
on the evening altars, and on doorsills of cratered homes,
also had no use for the scraps and bits
because, in their opinion, they looked good without them.
Since all things naturally return to their source,
these snags and tatters arrived, with immigrant uncertainty,
in the United States. It was almost home.
So, now, one can sometimes see a friend or a famous man talking
with an extra pair of lips glued and yammering on his cheek,
and this is why handshakes are often unpleasant,
why it is better, sometimes, not to look another in the eye,
why, at your daughter's breast thickens a hard keloidal scar.
After the war, with such Cheshire cats grinning in our trees,
will the ancient tales still tell us new truths?
Will the myriad world surrender new metaphor?
After our war, how will love speak?

...Forsan et haec olim meminisse juvabit.

   — AENEID, *Book I, line 203*

...Someday, perhaps, it will help to remember these things.

   — *Aeneas, to his crew of survivors, after the Trojan War.*

PART TWO

Riding Westward

Hence is't, that I am carryed towards the West
This day, when my Soules forme bends towards the East.
— *John Donne, "Goodfriday, 1613. Riding Westward"*

HEADING OUT WEST

All evening, below a sprig of yarrow,
by creekwater plunging through willow roots,
a cricket preened its song in our yard.

Down by the back eddy spinning with whirligigs,
I watched a fox pause from lapping up water
to lift a delicate paw and scratch
at redmites itching the root of its ear.

Then, as the sun ignited the willow stand
a blackbird flapped off a branch,
crossing shadowy fields like a thought.

All evening as crickets called, I creaked
a rocker on our paint-peeled porch,
sipped whisky, watched mist and fireflies
fill up the meadow, and considered
– long before I was a father –
my fellow Americans, the funny business of being married,
my deadly job and the jobs that would follow,
and all I could think of as I sat there
– safe from harm, steadily employed, happily married –
was how to get away.

                    At morning, I left,
hopping a ride west on the interstate, past
the cauldrons of Pittsburgh, its choked air,
past HoJos, Exxons, Arbys, Gulfs,
in the yammer and slam, the drone of trucks,
past the little lives that always are there,
past locusts chirring in a Tennessee graveyard,
past kudzu, pecans, then yucca and sage,

past armadillos scuttling off the berm of the highway,
…all the while wondering just what I was doing,
not sure where I was going; less sure, why.
But standing there, hanging out my thumb,
squinting at the stream of oncoming cars.

HITCH-HIKING AND LISTENING TO
MY CB WALKIE-TALKIE

In Questa, Chicanos shot four Anglo bikers.
Roared in on Harleys; rolled out under sheets.

In Boulder, an Indian buck-knifed a bartender.
Zigged, I guess, when he should've zagged.

At Rock Springs, my CB buzzed with double trouble;
On Friday, a cop at Green River wasted a narc.

Next night, at the Teddy Bear Inn, some girl
shot a guy through his nose. Oh, why am I in Wyoming?

At dawn in Salt Lake City, I heard swallows
chittering below a bridge, as light washed the Big Dipper.

And then ol' Captain Coors was honking with that Sugarlips
about the cabbie blown away by his fare.

Outside of Reno, I was riding in a big Peterbilt
when the trucker waved a snubnose at my head.

Just to let me know, you know. He didn't shoot.
But it makes you wonder about the living and the dead.

Late at night, when radio waves skip across States,
you can hear ricochets from Maine to L.A.

STORY

The guy picked me up north of Santa Fe
where the red hills, dotted with piñon,
loop down from the Divide into mesas and plain.
I was standing out there – just me, my pack,
and the gila monsters – when he hauled his Buick
off the road in a sputter of cinders and dust.
And got out, a gray-bearded, 6-foot, 300-pounder,
who stretched and said, "Do you want to drive?"
So I drove and he told me the story of his life.

How his father was a Russian Jew who got zapped
by the Mob during Prohibition, how he quit school
at fifteen and got a job as a DJ in Detroit,

how he sold flatware on the road and made a mint,
how he respected his wife, but didn't love her,
how he hit it big in radio and TV, how he fell in love,
how he found himself, at fifty, in intensive care
where his wife, his kids, his girlfriend, and his rabbi

huddled in silence about his bed when his doctor
came in and whispered that maybe he ought to ask
the wife and the girlfriend to alternate visits

'because it wasn't too good for his heart.'
"What about your kids?" I asked. "What do they do?"
"My daughter runs our store. My son is dead."
He studied a distant peak and didn't continue.
"What did he die of?"
                    "He died of suicide.
No, that's not right... Nixon killed him.
My son was a sweet kid, hated guns and violence

and then, during that fucking war, he hijacked a plane
and flew it to Cuba. He shot himself in Havana."
He watched the peak, then grinned and said,
"Brave little fucker, wasn't he?"

RIDING WESTWARD

You know that something's not quite right.
Perhaps the town is one of those
which marks its name and elevation
on a water tower stuck up on a hill.
Or maybe the hill itself declares the name
in whitewashed stones set just behind the town.
The big thing is the grain elevators.
The blacktop runs straight into them
just as country roads point to steeples
in Protestant towns along the Rhine.
But these tall towers are filled with wheat,
with corn and oats and rye, not hymns
to the stern father who sends us to the fields
or bids us read his Book before we eat,
who shuts our eyes in calms of beastlike sleep.

This poem is no tract for Jesus.
No fewer evils or epiphanies of joy
rise up here than did in Europe, which these
good farmers left because it was a grave.
Still one wonders. What was all this for,
the grizzled duffer in the John Deere cap asks
as he shuffles to Main Street's secondhand sale.
Rubble of shoes in cardboard boxes. And boots,
old button boots, a pile of iron peaveys
which rolled cottonwoods down from the river,
the forest long since cleared. Cracked photos
of a jackrabbit hunt, the creatures piled high
in heaps before the log-and-sod schoolhouse.

I mean, he asks, as he tweaks his balls
through the hole in his right jean pocket,

why did they do this? What was it for?
Doves perch on a wire above the dusty road.
Swallows sweep into a storefront eave.
A clump of orange lilies closes with the day.
A CB chatters in a parked Ford truck
its back bed loaded up with bales of hay:
"We got a Kojak with a Kodak takin' pictures
…he done a flip-flop on the superslab."
The pickup's empty; the owner's in the bar.

The rightest place to worry all this out
is at the first dead farmhouse outside town.
Sit there on the stoop's blistered boards
as swallows chitter towards their roosts,
the fat sun sinking in reddish pollen haze
beyond the silos, beyond the tasseled fields.

CROSSING WEST NEBRASKA,
LOOKING FOR BLUE MOUNTAIN

Where can one find the real Blue Mountain?
Inside the Blue Mountain at Waggoner's Gap,
is there another, pulsing cool azure light?
Can one drive west and find Blue Mountain?
Will anyone ever live there but me?
Some say that Blue Mountain is very small
and is rocking in the zion of a waterbead.
They claim to find it everywhere, even in clouds
of atmospheric dust snapping with strontium
and settling on the grasslands this evening.
Although Blue Mountain is only as large as a thought,
its sides drop off into dark crags; its steep slopes
are smooth as glass; its aspect is discouraging.
But from its peak, one can see everything clearly:

In humming fields, beetles, aphids, weevils, ants.
Fox pups frisking in bluebells before their burrow.
A naked boy and girl dogpaddling an inner tube
in bayou waters, off a levee near Big Mamou.
Subterranean rocks grinding in the San Andreas Fault.
A Malay fisherman, perched on a spit of rock off Penang,
hurling a circling net into surf at sunset.
A bloated mare giving foal in a clover field in Kent.
A blindfolded teenager, shoeless, slumped against a tree
as the firing squad walks off in Montevideo.
Missiles hidden like moles in Siberian silos.
A black man, in red cotton shirt and khaki pants, his skin
alive with protozoan welts, sipping coffee in a Congo shop.
An eel sliding through a corpse's yellowed ribs
in a Mekong swamp where frogs croak and egrets fish.
Ice sparkling the coats of hundreds of reindeer with
steaming nostrils, crossing a Lapland river under a moon.

As I pass in the dark through this sleeping town
the only creatures moving on Main Street are moths.
Spinning orbits about the lamps, they fall and die.
Their husks rustle like leaves in the fluorescent light.
Were they flying to Blue Mountain? Am I there?

SITTING ON BLUE MOUNTAIN, WATCHING THE BIRDS FLY SOUTH AND THINKING OF ST. JULIEN RAVENEL CHILDS

If the new is, or shall be, better,
purer, braver or higher, it will be well.
This is the tale of the old and it is done.
  — Mrs. St. Julien Ravenel, CHARLESTON

In a state of hysteria, the birds flap south.
Cowbirds, grackles, blackbirds, starlings
wink through the twilight in wavering lines
which break to tumble on stubbled cornfield
and woods which shrill with manic birds.
They flutter in branches, jostle and peck,
shuffle scaly claws along the boughs; nudge,
nestle, then tuck their heads in sleep.
At dawn, the flock will rise with shrieks,
scatter up, circle, and shake themselves south.
All night, katydids will chatter in the elms
as a last cricket plies its torpid trills.

Are these birds worth a whole stanza? Sure,
they point our noses south; our hearts, to memory.
I see them beady-eyed and ragtag, carpetbagging
through bright skies, over tobacco sheds
and broken levees, foggy marshes, old rice swamps,
past Moultrie's Fort on Sullivan's Island
where his rubbery palmetto-log stockade
swallowed grapeshot, bounced back British cannon,
past Sumter nearly flooded by the Bay,
to Charleston where the Ashley and Cooper rivers
"join to form the Atlantic," to Charleston
whose citizens, "like the Chinese, eat rice

and worship ancestors," and when they die
"go to Heaven and live on Legare Street."
Over mucky creeks and glints of cotton fields
my mind flies south with these raucous birds.

To you, old duffer, dreaming always of the past...
of a family of painters, planters, writers:
Your grandfather was a surgeon to slaves
and invented a submarine, *The Little David,*
which shunted like a squid off the Battery,
fired once at the Yankees and retired from the war.
Your grandmother described the city's fall.
The blockade, bombardment, and burning mansions,
Charleston's streets littered with window glass
as women and slaves saved what remained.
In 1922, you soldiered in Santo Domingo.
With Marines led by a latter General Lee
you chased bandits through riverine jungles
and saved the cane crop for a New York bank.
Your own interests were burned by Sherman
in a South sundered long before your birth.
These thoughts are as near as the pack of Camels
which you smoke on your porch on drizzly afternoons
as live oaks drip with autumn rain off the ocean
and the years wash like waves on a sandbar.
Last summer you floated off Folly Beach
and took in plays and opera at Spoleto,
sporting an ancient white tuxedo
yellowed like an old magnolia bloom.
The past is large-petaled and fades slowly.

We live in a world with a simple sense of use
that doesn't include poetry and musings.
Your thoughts are useless like poetry:
the tale of the better, purer, braver, higher.

You could be my brother, as well as granddad,
for the world would count us equally useless.
But I won't turn back from writing poems
or watching birds sail past Blue Mountain,
and you can't turn away from contemplating:
malarial swamps and stacks of sugarcane,
the crumbling piazza of your Georgian house,
a bag of sutures and rusting scalpels,
cavalry hooves clattering across a trestle
then splashing off into brackish swamp.

You may wonder, reading this as rains patter
the live oak twisted and huge in your yard,
where these yankees get all their presumption,
but I can tell, St. Julien, I can tell
by traces of indigo flowering in your thoughts
that Blue Mountain has sunk like an Atlantis
deep in your riverine, dynastic mind.

DEER KILL

The deer was down in a bed of maple leaves,
leaves dappled red, like blood, in the evening.
Grabbed the spindly hocks and heaved, rolling
the heavy doe on her back. Her eyes still clear.

Cut through the leaking web of nipples,
opening the belly like a burlap sack.
The blade's razor edge nicked her stomach bag
venting a stink of fermenting grass.

Freed the livid sheath from the red walls.
Her blood pumped out. From a severed tube.
In a scalding pool. In the great rib cage.
Heart, fatter than a hand, soapy to touch.

Pink rags of huge, shattered lungs.
Dropped liver out onto scratchy leaves.
Shook loose her stomach, bladder, and bowels.
Cleaved the pelvic ring with an ax.

Hand in the clean womb of the doe,
wet and white like chicken fat.
Threw a fist of it across the stream
rilling over stones under the chill moonlight.

Dabbed leaves in blood and stuck them to my face.
Screamed "wolf" at the moon; moon said, "man."

CHASING OUT THE DEMONS

for Tim Buckley

A bad case. Alone in the canyon,
screaming and charging a dirtbike
at the sandstone cliffs, he squinted
behind his wire-rim glasses
as the bugs splashed green and he bucked
across cottonwood roots and rubble
at breakneck speed, on a whining bike,
skidding to stops at the canyon walls.

At night, zipped in a sleeping bag,
he squirmed like a chrysalis under the moon
while the wind searched the willows
and the creek plunked into little pools
where trout batted at fireflies.

The two Indians came in his sleep:
two ghosts, pulses of wind and moonlight,
squatting beside him on the balls of their feet.
He shouted when the woman smoothed his hair.
And then they were gone and he cried.
Sobbed hard because it was goodbye,
goodbye to the spirit that raged in him by day
and now was traveling across the canyon creek
led off by the ghosts of two Indians
who had come to calm him.

He sat up that night by the dark cold water,
wrapped in a blanket, listening to the creek,
breaking his reverie only once
to cup his hands and draw to his lips
the moon rocking on the clear water.

JOURNEY IN THE DESERT

1 The Stone Lions

Surging the walls of the winding creek canyon
the old river shaved a smooth face in the stone,
each lava bubble a cave; each cave: a pueblo.
Crows, railing at humans for thousands of years,
circled the tourists scaling long ladders,
poking down kivas where Indians once sat like moles
and invited the earth to feed Spirit and Bone.
High above on the opposite cliff, a trail turns off
crossing the mesa through scraggly piñon
towards canyons too fickle with water for maize.
At Alamo Canyon, a drop and a Park sign:

> You are on the rim of Alamo Canyon. The
> Canyon here is 400 ft. deep. You should
> not cross unless you have: 1. at least
> one pint of water per person, 2. sturdy
> boots and a hat to protect you from the
> sun, and 3. better than average health.

Some miles farther on lies a ruined village,
now crumbled adobe and cairns of rocks,
shards, chips of obsidian, all crowned by cactus.
Nearby is a ring of great, raised-up stones
with a gate so that spirits may gather and go.
In the center, a pair of carved lions crouch,
bellies in dust, always ready to leap,
but corralled by a hedge of bleached antler prongs.
Flint-bits and shards have been cast to the lions.
The arrow shall fly and the cup brim water.

2 Kachina

Canyons, mesas, buttes, and chaparral.
A place so dry a cough can start a cloud;
terrain so odd, without events or acts,
a rock or circling crow might seem a sign,
a sheet of rain escorted by the sun
moves like a girl, sent by gods to dance,
whose beaded skirt of raindrops shot with light
will brush the canyon walls and fill up pools
thrilling songbirds thirsting in the dust.
Sheltered in a cave, I watch her pass
and wonder who and why and where she's gone;
and doubt, as in our lives or with a love,
if what I've seen and felt took place at all.
But trust these dripping leaves and trickling spells,
the human augured in the magpie's splash.

3 At Capulin Canyon

Night fell deep in the chilled-off canyon;
birds rustled in willows and oaks; were hushed
by the little creek's loudening chatter and rill.

Hidden in a cove of cottonwoods, I dozed
while sprinkles of stars circled the Pole Star.
The moon lifted over the eastern cliff wall.

The wind sailed in the tops of the pines.
Later, a snort and the stamping of hooves
startled me up as some great beast
crashed through the creek in a clatter of stones.

At daybreak, I spotted a lone horse grazing
in dry chaparral. I stalked the big stallion.
His coat slate gray. Dusted white. He stared,

flicked ears at my whistle, then galloped off
pounding up pumice at the caldera rim.
Coronado, Lame Dog, Two Moons, Price,
your revenant horse is lost in arroyos.

4 Painted Cave

This new Philosophy calls all else in doubt.
  – John Donne

Not really a cave, but, as Bandelier said,
"a grand portal of volcanic tuff,"
a massive vault in the basalt cliff
overlooking a wide canyon floor, strewn
with pocked boulders, a broken lava flow,
spiny cholla cactus, and stunted junipers.
And here Indians cut a ladder in the stone
to paint a roof with worries of their world:
the Spaniards' church at Santa Fe, a cross,
a bell, an armored man, horses, deer,
Indians striding with woven shields,
a bucket-headed god with a bird's blank eyes.
Were these paintings spiritual complaint?
Sad attempts to rule a hostile place?
And if their world was broken by greater force,
what can we say of ours: pulled into empty space
where galaxies writhe in igneous fury
to produce a living cell as part, their part,
of an elaborate practical joke.
The conquistadors have fallen from their mounts

and wander these wastes in search of water.
And if the desert gods loaned them a cave,
what would they paint? A plane, a clock,
blank sky, empty sea, the stalking atomic ghost.

5 Wedding in the Desert

A huge curtain of cloud torn down
spilling rain and sunfall into the desert
onto a horned toad squatting with bald eye
near a fish-hook cactus. The bright droplets
stutter in the dust by its head. It blinks.
High above, out of the lip of light cascading
from the raincloud, a man is falling,
smaller than a gnat, falling through the skylight,
swelling enormously as he tumbles to earth
to alight on the mesa, the bare mesa
where at night a blue lamp is always burning.

*

Toward dawn, two nimbus clouds drifted in,
the larger – trailing down tendrils of rain
like a Portuguese man-o'-war – began to pulse
with lightning, brightening its belly
like a huge lantern, arcing a jagged streak
to ignite the smaller cloud.
Pulsing and flaring, striking each other,
dragging the earth with rain,
they drifted off over the mountains.
All about them the sky was clear.

WALKING DOWN INTO CEBOLLA CANYON

Then, truly unhappy, terrified by Fate, wearied
by the empty sky, Dido prayed for death.
  — AENEID, *Book IV, line 450*

1 Everything about us, for better or worse,
   we make ourselves, with marvelous exceptions:
   The snow peaks rinsed in rose light
   at dusk on the Sangre de Cristo range.
   The bleached, broken jaw of a mule deer,
   its teeth scattered among cactus wreaths
   beside the trail, down from the mesa,
   where the river stammers against volcanic
   rocks and pools where spooked trout skim
   through aspen leaves tumbling in clear water.

2 The river cut through centuries of rock
   to this time when all assertions are suspect,
   to this century when assurances are mute,
   when we, deserted like Dido before her pyre
   or Raleigh pacing The Lie in the Tower,
   look up to see "a wearying, empty sky"
   and gag on words like sour meats
   stewed in the stomach of a haggis sheep.
   So, pity the poets, whose work is words,
   reduced to blather or fiery silences
   when God who breathed the Word expired.

3 This vast rubble offers its one blessing:
   everything it says is true – parched mesa,
   willow water, fox skull, circling raven,
   tarantula, deer turd, singing wren.
   One wanders down past living metaphors.

Where life is threatened, no lies are told.
Under a blank sky one clambers past
collapsed ledges clustered with paintbrush,
blue saxifrage and hooded columbine.
Small. Alone. No better than a bug.

4 If one accepts these terms, he takes his place
offered all along by the ribboned stream
calling up from the bouldered canyon floor,
to stand here at dusk and stare at spilling water
near a wren jigging on a laved slab
in the river which leaps through lunar wastes
where trout, coyote, magpie, cougar, prosper
in the innocence which humans find in love.
So I bring back the water's benediction:

"The streams we play in flow sweet water.
Anyone might drink here and be refreshed.
All day, sunlight strikes the river clear,
At dusk, the current ripples with a moon.
Love like water makes the canyons bloom."

KATE AND GARY'S BAR,
RED RIVER, NEW MEXICO

Just over the mountains from Eagle Nest
where the glacial maw ground out a valley
and oceans of gold aspens surge around steep
boulder fields and islands of evergreens and
the collapsing ghost town where hippies hole up
you come to Red River: a string of bars
and curio shops, all pine planks and logs.
The river rattles rocks behind the town.
Farther on, towards Questa where the Rockies open
to volcanic plains, a huge gray slag heap
slides toward the river from the molybdenum mine.
The town makes no claims on eternity,
a mere moment in the granite gorge
shadowed by whistling crags and forests
beside a river carving out canyons
eating its way to the sea.

Kate's son drove me into town,
picked me up off the road from Questa,
so I had her roast beef special and a beer.
She pulled a chair from the edge of the dance floor,
watched my Adam's apple bob with beer and studied
my backpack and sleeping bag leaning by the door.
"What do you do, anyway?" she asked. "You're no drifter."
"I write poetry," I said. She smiled,
and pushed her bifocals back up her nose.
"I knew you did something like that.
Grace," she called behind the bar
to the long-legged girl setting up drinks,
"bring our friend another Coors."

DADDY OUT HITCH-HIKING AT 3:00 A.M.

Finally it was just me, and the katydids
cranking out nightsongs in clumps of willows
by a barn roofed in moonlight, by a ryefield
luminous with dew. I stepped off the highway
ribboning out through the valley. Walked
through wet weeds to a pond gathering vapors.

Angels see the way I saw that night
when only large shapes loomed
and all my thoughts were laid aside
as I searched the night opening before me
and soul shuffled out of self to sing
with katydids chattering in murky trees.

All beasts are kind with divine instruction.
The paired ducks slept beneath their wings.
Minnows wavered in the moon-charmed creek
where a muskrat hunched and licked its paws
listening like me to insects calling
searching and calling at the end of summer.

This is what Daddy was doing
the August you were born.
Wandering off alone on highways
walking off highways into the night
calming a head loud with the past
listening to things that make a song.

PASSING THROUGH ALBUQUERQUE

At dusk, by the irrigation ditch
gurgling past backyards near the highway,
locusts raise a maze of calls in cottonwoods.

A Spanish girl in a white party dress
strolls the levee by the muddy water
where her small sister plunks in stones.

Beyond a low adobe wall and a wrecked car
men are pitching horseshoes in a dusty lot.
Someone shouts as he clangs in a ringer.

Big winds buffet in ahead of a storm,
rocking the immense trees and whipping up
clouds of dust, wild leaves, and cottonwool.

In the moment when the locusts pause and the girl
presses her up-fluttering dress to her bony knees
you can hear a banjo, guitar, and fiddle

playing "The Mississippi Sawyer" inside a shack.
Moments like that, you can love this country.

PORTAL

The sun's up in El Paso
rising over the red volcanic plain,
igniting the dry Rockies, setting ablaze
the eastern walls of our towered city
at the edge of the other world.
Where Rockies become the worn Chihuahuas
and the muddy Rio Grande churns by fencing
strung with razor wire. Where the sun
glints off a water truck bumping through
the tarpaper barrios in Juarez, flares off
the International Bridge already jammed
with old Fords and Chevys, with packed pickups,
jornaleros on foot with their bundles,
the lame, the illiterate, the bent and weary,
walking to Texas for a day's pay.

A boy, fifteen, wispy moustache, straw hat,
stops amid the traffic on the bridge.
Holds in hand a card of the Madonna
in princess gown, tiara, attendant angels.
He whispers to the picture. Shuffles on.

AGUA FRIA Y LAS CHICHARRAS

1 Alhambra

When the voice of the Prophet crossed the Sahara
clattering out from mud-walled souks with Berber horsemen,
it carried swiftly through those wastes, for as the Arabs say,
in the desert there is nothing but the presence of Allah.
And in Granada, below snow peaks rinsing in sunlight,
at the Alhambra, Al Qal'a al-Hamara, the Architect's Garden,
the Moors made Him visible everywhere, in horseshoe portals
and sandstone ramparts stamped with the Key,
in icy fountains teased out from the rock
looping toward heaven, collapsing in pools, plunging down
stairwells banistered in liquid light. *Quien quiere agua?*
the water-carriers sang, *agua mas fria que nieve.*
In the spill of water, the signature of god.
And outside the citadel of Allah, in paradisiacal parks,
the locusts calling at the edge of wilderness.

2 Arroyo Hondo, New Mexico

He pitched his camp inside a canyon
where willows twist on boulders shoved up beside the creek.
Poplars shook out sunlight after a rain. By the dead fire
lay a charred bean can and a plastic bag spilling out flour.
In the creek, a Coors six-pack; a pint of half-and-half.
He had some clothes draping a rock, a bedroll
sprawled on soggy blankets. By that, an empty suitcase.
I found him staring at the stream.
He looked about thirty, said he lived near Denver,
put up sheetrock for a living, was leaving for L.A.
He said he had been to her place in town. It was empty.

He stood outside her house until he heard echoes gather,
saw shapes move, imagined her children's yelps,
her laughter, her husband's arms around her
as they leaned against the sink and kissed.
The marigolds she left behind still glimmered in the shade
below the cottonwood where, high up, locusts called.
He said it was like he saw her reading by the window
then putting down the book to stare at him staring in.
Like a ghost watching a ghost. He offered me a beer
saying he had come here through a valley of lies
with no guide but hunger for her. No Christ, no cop, no book,
no mother or father, no flag, and the few friends he counted
were gone and God knows where. She too was gone for good.
He wanted me to know about a lake,
dry, some sixty miles up north in Colorado
where Indians emerged as men, led out, led up
from Sipapu, the Underworld, upon pulses of song
by Kokopelli, The Hump-Backed Flute Player, the Locust God,
whose song can heal. We sipped his beer and listened
to whines of locusts falling on the creek.

3 Rosale's

Ro-*sah*-le's. Just north of Taos in El Prado
past the feed sign for henscratch: $5.50/50 lbs.
You go there if you're hungry and it's late.
Rosale's a Mexican from Juarez, does a big business
from midnight to dawn when all the drunks
and lounge lizards stumble in as bars shut down.

So everyone's ugly and stiff in the eye sockets
because it's too late to get laid, because
their lives stink. So they fight.
Once the cops raided and took away a lot of guns
but I never heard of anyone *dying* there

so I go…and one night I saw an awful fight
with four drunks kicking this squirmy Anglo
who had been coldcocked while eating his eggs
and lay groaning below a table, everyone just watching
until the big girl in the blue smock waddled out
from the kitchen, screamed, and shoved them out.
No fun in that fight at all.

When I left, dawn was cracking behind the mountains
and high up I saw the bright porpoise brow of a jet
streaming east, nose silvery with sunlight
above the darkened earth. The plane was a comfort
darting across the open sky like a clear thought,
it said, "Look around. The signs are all about you
even in a sorry brawl in a Mexican café."
Each spring, I thought, they clean the ditches,
the *aquecias*, of leaf muck and debris.
Each must marvel when waters spill again
and cottonwoods shimmer in a web of poems
as redwings bob and whistle the branches
and canyons fill with the locust's song.
Oh, the hunger for words pure as clear water
that shall slake the pain of our parched tongues
and, splashed against our brows, shall let us see.
In such a moment, locusts reinstruct our rapture.
Cold and mute, we are led up from dark worlds
into a sunstruck glade loud with rilling water.
At the song's start, the raw tongue stammers out
an urge toward paradise, a version of ease.

ELISEO'S CABIN, TAOS PUEBLO

Yellow alfalfa banks the rutted lane
that winds in under the bedstead gate
latched with loops of baling wire.
Horseskulls bleach on fenceposts
running down through sagebrush
to the cabin snug by the sandy creek.
Pieces of plows hang from the cedars
along with barn hinges, tractor chains,
and a rusted-out kettle. A buffalo hide
drapes a lodgepole wedged in willows.
The cabin's covered in sweetpea vines,
blossoms tumbling out bees.
Eliseo has set his cot outside
near an iron pot brimming peonies.

Lying alone at night, watching
stars shake, hearing the creek talk,
he remembers before there was a camp
and his father would come here to watch
thunderheads collapse on the prairie
and drag sweeps of rain across arroyos.
Worried about the old man sleeping on the ground
he sawed planks and hauled them up by buckboard
rocking to the meadow on wheels that smelled of sage.

Now old himself he comes to his cabin
to heat chili and bread on the wood stove
to sleep by the creek or sit by a spruce
whittling birds for grandchildren.
In the dark, he hears his ponies graze
across the fern-crowded creek

where fireflies flare like memories
and his father and grandchildren's voices
rise from the cold traveling water.

STUDYING THE SEASONS ON BLUE MOUNTAIN

1 Summer

Trying to find Blue Mountain
was like searching for a cricket in a field.
I'd drive out, following my best directions,
and meander from noon to nightfall
in bogs and cornfields and tangly woods.
My car would get stuck; the battery'd die,
I'd walk to a farmhouse to call for a tow.
Back in town, I'd sit at the bar with a beer,
wondering why the locals were lying,
studying my maps for yet another try,
slapping mosquitoes whining at my ear.

A firefly blinking on the lip of a leaf
finally led me to higher ground.
Slight change…still the flatlands,
but already I caught the incense of pine needles
and saw the moon huge in the thinner air.
So I kept going until I got to the ledge
overlooking Phantom Lake and the ghost town.
My breath condensed in the cool mountain breeze.
My nostrils seemed to pour out moonlight.

2 Fall

I came back to chop wood. My razory ax
rang out in the lonely clearing.
My first swings sent deer bounding off,
white tails wagging, hooves scattering dry leaves.

I'd take the logs and roll them down the hill,
crushing blackened ferns, frozen moths,
dead spores and leaf dust swirling on the wind
as the bald trees rocked and creaked
and Blue Mountain shone cold and bare,
planetary, like a lump of coal.

3 Winter

Bright sun and the east slope hushed by snow.
The thickets hooded. The bedraggled pines
dipped and shuddered free their boughs.
My bootlaces caught on blackberry canes.
Warm air steamed from a rabbit's hole.
Below the white traceries of wild vines,
where purply, wizened grapes stained the snow,
two grouse thundered off, spraying snowflakes.
I plodded on. Deer tracked the drifts.
Then, out of nowhere, large and silent,
a shadow swept the snow before my boots
as a hawk cleared the treetops and sailed
over the brilliant valley where chimneys puffed,
a dog barked, and children sledded down a hill.
Where did it fly from? Cave? A cliff nest?
A secret perch where winter hawks roost.
Words stir. Get up. And fly.

4 Spring

A spring seeps from the warm side of the mountain,
collects in a pool in the limestone rocks,
spills into a shallow creek.
I went there in April, the earth spongy,
Spring Beauties trembling their white cups.

In the valley, spears of skunk cabbage reared
green ram horns in the mucky woods
and ferns unfurled in the bogs.
But on Blue Mountain I found the spring
choked with dead leaves, overgrown with briars,
marked only by a trickling in the rocks.
I plunged my hand through the icy water
and pushed away the soggy leaves; below,
in the clear pool of pure water,
a speckled trout darted alone and free.

LOVERS NEAR JEMEZ SPRINGS

Across the canyon creek
bridged with bubbled ice
snow filled their tracks

through aspens
up the whitening hill
along the power-line path

falling, filling their footprints
where they halted by the doe
stretched stiff in the snow

where they worked on
through dusted blackberry canes
into hushed pines

to the cattle pond
drained by muskrats
and sprouting dead cattails

where her footsteps
went to the snow-drifted bank
and his scuffed the glaze

over the pond's heart
as they talked. Snow filled
their footsteps where they came together.

*

Spring in these woods
is all fern swale, teaberry,
Indian pipes and paintbrush

the doe, a dried rug
on a rack of bones,
the brambles; flowering.

The pond rustles green sheaves
as redwings bob
in wild alfalfa

and peepers keen the bog.
All this occurs without her.
He comes here alone.

And where leaves unfurl
from oak and cottonwood,
he sees instead a snowfall.

And where chokecherry shakes
in tiny blossoms,
he sees a falling snow.

A TINY BIRD

A tiny bird with red feathers,
a tiny bird with black beak
drinks up the lotus pond day by day.
Perhaps I must leave you.

translation of a Vietnamese folk poem

SNOWBOUND

Tragedies of clouds still stumble over us
stalled in cars and tractor-trailers
along the highway blocked at a mountain pass,
but now a track team from a chartered bus
has shoved a van past a jack-knifed trailer
and so, after long hours, a lane is cleared
for all the bickering parents and bratty kids
for truckers zonked on speed and nattering on CB's
for the long-hauler with straggly hair and no front teeth
who struck out in the snow to straighten things out
and who stomped back angry, for the snoozing salesmen,
for the old folks too shy to pee by the road
for the teenagers yelling in hormonal fits
for the wailing babies, for the diabetic
shooting his thigh behind a fogged windshield
for the lovers feeling lucky at being trapped together
and, oh, just wishing it were night,
for all of us now inching forward in a glittering line
resuming our lives under a sweep of clearing sky.

THREE WAYS OF LOOKING AT SPARROWS

Bede wrote it was a *spearwa*
that brought an afterlife to Saxon kings
as the friar spoke in the timbered hall
and no one listened until a sparrow
fluttered in the east loft, then flew out the west,
thus showing a figure for the soul.

Catullus saw its naughty side,
nestled between his girlfriend's breasts
and gently stroked, the little beak
stropping its lady's pretty thumb.
Whenever Clodia fucked her brother,
her little bird would chirp.

Then there's this little guy:
your average citizen sparrow
pecking about the chicken pen
for cracked corn, scared of beaks,
scratching, all hop and hope,
pretty much taking it as it comes.

PEYOTE VILLANELLE

Watch out for this one, USA.
  – Peyote Road Chief, Taos, N.M.

1 The trail lost, he looked about
across the bouldered canyon floor.
In desert wastes the soul cries out

then echoes back in dusty shouts,
wavering ghosts in chaparral.
The trail lost, he looked about

the creekbed where he shot his mount.
Horseflies sucked the splash of gore.
In desert wastes the soul cries out.

Though no one heard, he called out loud.
Snakes uncurled in a cave's cool door.
The trail lost, he looked about

and shuffled forth, dry in mouth,
aching for home and green remorro.
In desert wastes the soul cries out

in blind canyons, under blank sky. Scouting
for water, throat parched and sore,
with the trail lost he looked about
desert wastes. The soul cries out.

2 "Come eat peyote and you shall live."
The woman waved and called him on.
"A god has made this road a gift."
She crossed the arroyo and came to him
cloaked in light and shakes of rain.
"Come, eat peyote and you shall live."

Her fingers brushed his blistered lips.
She talked like water; touched like dawn.
A god had made the road a gift.

For in that realm of scorpion and snake
his soul cried out and the woman came
fashioned from light and veiled in rain.
He followed a god through desert wastes.

THE GIFT OF MORNING WATER

After the long night with a cold wind riffling the scrim of the tee-pee, lit like a lantern on the deserted prairie, a night of chills in the small of the back, aches in crossed legs, after all the hours of chanting from Indians and Anglos, after their drumming on the iron kettle stretched with hide, its water-filled belly bellowing when tipped, after the prayers sung for forgiveness, for guidance from the grandfather peyote on the crescent of sand, after chewing bitter buttons, swallowing dry powder, after the drumming and the singing and the sweet sage thrown on the dazzling fire, as the embers died and dawn finally rinsed the top of the tent, the Road Chief, an elderly Tiwa who throughout the night had asked "him" to show us the right road, said: "A woman is coming with morning water. Listen to her. She is your mother."

An old Pueblo woman crawled through the tent flap, short of breath and shoving before her on the teepee sand a steel bucket, water sloshing, ladle clanking, and I turned with exhaustion, with disappointment, for all night long I had sat eating the "medicine," going out only once under the huge, roaring stars to take a leak and return, and nothing, really, had happened.

And then she spoke with puffy, tired lips, said, "You have done a good thing here tonight. Drink this water and be refreshed," and every syllable that came from her was perfectly the voice of my own mother, dead for many years. Stunned, and now weeping, I sat as the bucket came around to me, wept hard at hearing her voice again.

I have a friend in Vermont who, for a full week after his father's death, kept calling the family answering machine, just to hold a bit longer to his father's voice. And here I was made a gift I hadn't known how much I wanted, the voice that called my name the first morning of my life.

WORDS FOR THE DEAD

Alexandra Georgies Balaban, 1911–1978

What can one do in a poem about his mother
but record her gifts and deny her faults?
But not the way that undertakers work
with powder and rouge and cotton in the cheeks,
for they work with Flesh, not with Spirit.
What can one save in a poem about his mother?
Certainly not her life. Nor could the surgeon
who finished in her heart, hoping to hook
his little lure to teach her heart to beat.

Her children will consider her raising of children:
the years laid aside like laundry, her comforting us
on winter nights when our coal fire was banked
and ice froze our breaths on the insides of windows.
But what was it that she wanted for herself?
She said her girlhood wish was to sing contralto;
as she ironed clothes we heard her hum at tunes.
Later, with all the housework done, she'd read
a dime-store romance that would leave her with the blues.
Oh, she dreamed, and daydreamed, and was patient.

Into that peculiar silence which only parents have,
she retreated, and, now, she has entered it forever.
Surely that silence was the silence of her dreaming.
What did she think there? We will never know.
But if all things crave themselves more clearly,
we who issued from the cells of her body, whose
first pulses flexed with the rhythms of her heart,
are each partial flesh and seed of her craving
for wistful things. That are her. And will not die.

FOR MY SISTER IN WARMINSTER
GENERAL HOSPITAL

The two birds augured something strange.
First, I saved the blackpoll warbler
that piped twice as the cat pounced
and clawed the slapping wings.
No blood, but the bird couldn't fly.
It pecked my warm hands.
Slept the night in a bamboo creel.
When I took it out the next morning
it peeped before bounding to a hemlock,
cocked its head at me,
and then flew off to Argentina.

Then the junco sitting by the door.
I scooped it up, making my hands a nest.
When I let it loose later in the day
it bobbed away in the little arcs
that juncos make from bush to bush.
Two birds in the same day. Just exhausted.

I've heard of whole migrations blown off course,
looking for the Orkneys, lost in the Atlantic,
plummeting like hail onto a passing ship
where they flopped, faltered, and died.
All about, birds falling into swells.

So these auguries were for you, my sister,
asthmatic, gasping to flex your lungs
for ten days, or so I learned tonight.

When I was small and also could not breathe
you read me comics: Little Lulu and Scrooge McDuck

were our favorites. You read or made them up
while your skinny brother sat like a board in bed
and wheezed and panic widened in his eyes.

But I rested and flew off.
Thirty years later, you force your lungs for air.
Consider: whole flocks lost and blown into the sea.
Consider the sailors looking from that deck,
watching the waves engulf the keening birds.
It makes no sense; it only happens.

You be the bird that fell down exhausted,
that rested and took off, a bit later in the day.

A WOMAN ALONE ON THE ROAD

It's a risk and a bother
in this world that's still male
when around each bend may lie
ambushes of absurd encounters
and the streets fix her
with cold stares.
This woman alone on the road.
Her only defense
is her defenselessness.

She hasn't made from any man
a crutch, or wayside shelter.
She never walked over a man
as if he were a bridge.
She went off alone
to meet him as an equal
and to love him truly.

Whether she'll go far
or falter in the mud
or be blinded by horizons
she doesn't know. She's stubborn.
Even if rebuked along the way
her setting out itself
is accomplishment enough.
A woman alone on the road.
And yet she goes on
and does not stop.

No man can be as lonesome
as a woman on her own.

Before her the darkness
drops down a locked door.
A woman alone on the road
ought not go out at night.
The dawn sun, like a turnkey,
will unlock her horizons.

Still she goes on
even in the darkness
not glancing about in fear
but each step measuring her faith
in the Dark Man
with whom she's been threatened
for a long time.
Her steps echo on the paving
and stub against a stone.
A woman alone on the road:
quiet brave steps over a sad earth,
an earth which, against the stars,
is a woman alone on the road.

translated from the Bulgarian (with Alexandra Veleva)
of Blaga Dimitrova

THAT MAN

pissing off the front stoop
into the night, his urine
splattering the crusted snow,
is me. He listens
to his water and to the water
of the brook beyond the alders,
watching the oblate moon careen
above the India ink hemlocks
and hearing the brook nag: "Time
flows. Flowering times."
Because a girl he's begun to know
is now bathing in the tub,
he's skunked outside. Because
of that because. I've stepped outside.
I should go and introduce them,
if I could. But I too am baffled
by the moon rocking in the hemlocks,
by the moons rickling in the stream.

SOME THINGS THAT HAPPENED
BEFORE MY DAUGHTER'S BIRTH

1 A Poem Her Mother Wrote Me the Year I Was Away

Snow piles up these lonely nights.
This winter you are gone.
Knee-deep, February drifts choke
the railroad bed we walked in summer
edged by daisies and black-eyed susans.

From the woods Rangers drag out deer.
Ribs poke through their rusty coats.
The Rangers say "no forage." Too much snow.
The coldest winter in our century.

Fitting that we should be apart.
Powerful winds and hibernation of the soul.
Like the deer pawing for bark, I peel away
the crust of my own heart, pumping these days
in a white expanse, frozen every dawn,
as snow falls where we walked together.

2 My Reply

Sweetest love, I do not go
For weariness of thee...
   – John Donne

Let's say that I was called away
summoned by a voice I heard first as a boy
when belly down on the cool bank
I looked in the wrinkling water
at skeeters sculling tiny oars,

at a crayfish wading through willow roots
unraveling under clear ripples.
I was so still a woodthrush supped beside me.
So quiet, I dwelt with spotted newts.

"Come" is all that voice has ever said,
wet with ferns and mossy logs
with catbird cry and frog croak.
And when I followed I was always happy
reading delight in signatures of fish,
in moth glyphs scribbled beneath elm bark,
even though lonely; as now, for you.

What calls me away shall call me home.
I knew your voice before we met.
These journeys out, are journeys back.
Let's say my travels tend toward you.

FLYING HOME

for Tally, Age Three

So this is how the journey ends.
I'm sitting here in a Lottaburger
near Winchell's Donut, in Albuquerque
across the street from Miniature Golf
where a teen in tight jeans and Danskin top
twirls a putter, majorette-style.

Just over there is the 7-Eleven,
while over here, an Exxon and Skat.
Above the Sandias a thunderstorm
drops thunderbolts and drags the rain.
A wayward bird careens in sight,
blown by gusts and flapping wildly.

In two more days I fly back home.
When I scoop you up into a hug
you'll cry, "Don't crush me *bones!*"
My tiny guide to a wiser life.
Little wren who calls me home.

PART THREE

Viewing the New World Order

How we stood, in the early season, but at the end of the day,
In the yes of new light, but at the twice-lit hour..."
  — *Louise Bogan, "Short Summary"*

"And the locusts sang, way off in the distance."
  — *Bob Dylan, "Day of the Locust," from* NEW MORNING, *1970*

WORDS FOR MY DAUGHTER

About eight of us were nailing up forts
in the mulberry grove behind Reds's house
when his mother started screeching and
all of us froze except Reds – fourteen, huge
as a hippo – who sprang out of the tree so fast
the branch nearly bobbed me off. So fast,
he hit the ground running, hammer in hand,
and seconds after he got in the house
we heard thumps like someone beating a tire
off a rim   his dad's howls   the screen door
banging open   Saw   Reds barreling out
through the tall weeds toward the highway
the father stumbling after his fat son
who never looked back across the thick swale
of teazel and black-eyed susans until it was safe
to yell fuck you at the skinny drunk
stamping around barefoot and holding his ribs.

Another time, the Connelly kid came home to find
his alcoholic mother getting raped by the milkman.
Bobby broke a milk bottle and jabbed the guy
humping on his mom. I think it really happened
because none of us would loosely mention that
wraith of a woman who slippered around her house
and never talked to anyone, not even her kids.
Once a girl ran past my porch
with a dart in her back, her open mouth
pumping like a guppy's, her eyes wild.
Later that summer, or maybe the next,
the kids hung her brother from an oak.
Before they hoisted him, yowling and heavy
on the clothesline, they made him claw the creekbank
and eat worms. I don't know why his neck didn't snap.

Reds had another nickname you couldn't say
or he'd beat you up: "Honeybun."
His dad called him that when Reds was little.

*

So, these were my playmates. I love them still
for their justice and valor and desperate loves
twisted in shapes of hammer and shard.
I want you to know about their pain
and about the pain they could loose on others.
If you're reading this, I hope you will think,
Well, my dad had it rough as a kid, so what?
If you're reading this, you can read the news
and you know that children suffer worse.

*

Worse for me is a cloud of memories
still drifting off the South China Sea,
like the 9-year-old boy, naked and lacerated,
thrashing in his pee on a steel operating table
and yelling, "Đau. Đau," while I, trying to translate
in the mayhem of Tet for surgeons who didn't know
who this boy was or what happened to him, kept asking
"Where? Where's the pain?" until a surgeon
said, "Forget it. His ears are blown."

*

I remember your first Halloween
when I held you on my chest and rocked you,
so small your toes didn't touch my lap
as I smelled your fragrant peony head
and cried because I was so happy and because

I heard, in no metaphorical way, the awful chorus
of Sœur Anicet's orphans writhing in their cribs.
Then the doorbell rang and a tiny Green Beret
was saying trick-or-treat and I thought *oh oh*
but remembered it was Halloween and where I was.
I smiled at the evil midget, his map-light and night
paint, his toy knife for slitting throats, said,
"How ya doin', soldier?" and, still holding you asleep
in my arms, gave him a Mars Bar. To his father
waiting outside in fatigues I hissed, "You, shit,"
and saw us, child, in a pose I know too well.

I want you to know the worst and be free from it.
I want you to know the worst and still find good.
Day by day, as you play nearby or laugh
with the ladies at Peoples Bank as we go around town
and I find myself beaming like a fool,
I suspect I am here less for your protection
than you are here for mine, as if you were sent
to call me back into our helpless tribe.

SPRING-WATCHING PAVILION

A gentle spring evening arrives
airily, unclouded by worldly dust.
Three times the bell tolls echoes like a wave.
We see heaven upside down in sad puddles.
Love's vast sea cannot be emptied.
And springs of grace flow easily everywhere.
Where is nirvana?
Nirvana is here, nine times out of ten.

from the Vietnamese of Ho Xuan Huong

AT 4:00 A.M., ASLEEP

I wanted to shoot the jerk
whining his wheels on an ice patch
dragging me from sleep
even before sparrows screech the dawn
up from snow-crusted choirs of forsythia
between houses somehow asleep.
But maybe the jerk is a her not a him
some poor drudge who's finally had it
after a long night of shouts and slaps.

Maybe this suburb isn't the dead zone.
Maybe others are awake...some old guy
sitting up with arthritis, chain-smoking,
or a mother, leaning over a crib
stroking her child crackling with phlegm,
or some man fishing in a toilet bowl
as his wife sobs into her hands and he spoons up
the blood clot, the embryo sac, to take to the doctor
to see what went wrong.
                              Thinking these things
before falling back to sleep, I realized
I was called out into a field of compassion
into a universe of billions of souls, and
that was a messenger now driving away.

IN CELEBRATION OF SPRING

Our Asian war is over; others have begun.
Our elders, who tried to mortgage lies,
are disgraced, or dead, and already
the brokers are picking their pockets
for the keys and the credit cards.

In delta swamp in a united Vietnam,
a Marine with a bullfrog for a face,
rots in equatorial heat. An eel
slides through the cage of his bared ribs.
At night, on the old battlefields, ghosts,
like patches of fog, lurk into villages
to maunder on doorsills of cratered homes,
while all across the usa
the wounded walk about and wonder where to go.

And today, in the simmer of lyric sunlight,
the chrysalis pulses in its mushy cocoon,
under the bark on a gnarled root of an elm.
In the brilliant creek, a minnow flashes
delirious with gnats. The turtle's heart
quickens its taps in the warm bank sludge.
As she chases a Frisbee spinning in sunlight,
a girl's breasts bounce full and strong;
a boy's stomach, as he turns, is flat and strong.

Swear by the locust, by dragonflies on ferns,
by the minnow's flash, the tremble of a breast,
by the new earth spongy under our feet:
that as we grow old, we will not grow evil,
that although our garden seeps with sewage,

and our elders think it's up for auction — swear
by this dazzle that does not wish to leave us —
that we will be keepers of a garden, nonetheless.

FOR THE MISSING IN ACTION

Hazed with heat and harvest dust
the air swam with flying husks
as men whacked rice sheaves into bins
and all across the sun-struck fields
red flags hung from bamboo poles.
Beyond the last treeline on the horizon
beyond the coconut palms and eucalyptus
out in the moon-zone puckered by bombs
the dead earth where no one ventures,
the boys found it, foolish boys
riding buffaloes in craterlands
where at night bombs thump and ghosts howl.
A green patch on the raw earth.
And now they've led the farmers here,
the kerchiefed women in baggy pants,
the men with sickles and flails, chidren
herding ducks with switches – all
staring from a crater berm; silent:
In that dead place the weeds had formed a man
where someone died and fertilized the earth, with flesh
and blood, with tears, with longing for loved ones.
No scrap remained; not even a buckle
survived the monsoons, just a green creature,
a viny man, supine, with posies for eyes,
butterflies for buttons, a lily for a tongue.
Now when huddled asleep together
the farmers hear a rustly footfall
as the leaf-man rises and stumbles to them.

GRAVEYARD AT BALD EAGLE RIDGE

Solomon's seal, false and true,
Jewelweed, and Arrowroot.
Here swallows, snatching at bugs,
skirt the cornstalks' tassled tops
and dart above the sunken stones
of the hillside graveyard.

Farmers hold dearly to their dead:
the dead in childbirth, dead in war,
dead with sickness, dead with age.
Neatly as a kitchen garden,
they have tended the tombstones.
But, see, a bucktoothed woodchuck
burrows out a daughter's bones.
Will a tooth churn up? Cracked
wishbones of a child's hand?

Rainfogs lift off the valley
which the dead are set to view.
Cowbells clang in earshot, while
a white nag chomps amid the clover.
Looking out, the dead – the Shirks,
Browns, Gingerys, and Rines –
find their children green-haired,
socket-blind, and lying beside them.
In this year of our Lord,
a sparse generation tills the land.

HISSARLIK

*Such is the will of Zeus, who has laid many a proud city
in the dust, as he will yet lay others.*
 — ILIAD

This is the dust
of nine cities,
royal as the poppy,

each grown
over the sediment
of the last.

Here the dust of Achaeans
and of Priam's sons
mingles

with the shards and stones,
the bones – remnants
of slaves and lords.

Nine cities,
born in turn
upon the death mounds

of the former,
entombing themselves,
building this hill.

This is the hill
of Hissarlik where
the limbs of countless

entwine and dissolve
under the common earth
which we sift and shovel

into fluted ashcans
that lie empty now
like broken white columns.

HAIL TO THE CHIEF

When Claudius weighed the edict
giving his divine consent
to farting at the banquet table
years of conquest had fallen
since Cornelia's aristocratic jewels,
Tiberius and Gaius Gracchus,
misfortuned the Republic
with vague notions of equity
only to win for themselves
popularity and assassination.
A law to fart by is, surely,
as much a sign of the times
as Nero's nightly garden parties
lit by pitch-dipped Christians.
On the subject, Suetonius says little,
but, no doubt, certain patricians squawked
(as Rome met Parthian, Dacian, and Pict)
that the barbarian defeats had derived
from turning the Field of Mars
into a park of statuary; while others,
less loudly, griped about Cato's
fabulous and ill-gotten wealth.
But who can forget Tiberius?
the emperor dubbed "Callipedes"
in memory of that favorite mime
who played the long-distance runner
without ever taking a step.

LETTERS FROM ACROSS THE SEA

Here, where I must live among the barbarian Getæ,
it is enough to remain a poet. *
  – Ovid, EPISTULÆ EX PONTO

1 Pontus

A Turkish moon slides across the Sea
reaping crests that float ashore
where shellwash chatters like broken teeth
of mariners, still telling tales
of beasts which lurk below the depths,
storms in the straits and triremes lost.
From the seaside town where he was sent,
Ovid's statue stares across
sealanes never to bear him home.
Exiled for "a poem and an error."
Such clever rage Augustus wrought
in punishment simple yet complete:
to banish this poet and city man
forever, from Rome, from talk in Latin.
Today, we all live banished lives,
and which is worse, we wanderers ask,
exile in a foreign land or exile in one's own?
Through smogged cities, tramcars slam,
screech and spit electric sparks. At Tomis,
the waves wash whispers out to sea.

---

* *"Hoc, ubi vivendum est, satis est, si consequor arvo inter inhumanos esse*
  poeta Getas." Pontus and Fortuna were the gods of the city Tomis,
  now the Romanian Black Seaport of Constanţa, where Ovid's statue
  stands.

2 Fortuna

The Sea and Fortune rule this place.
Perhaps Augustus felt poetic flights
and chose this spot ironically,
thinking of the poet at his door
looking out and seeing only waves,
the Sea his fortune; Fortune, the sea.
You knew this as your keel rode east
booming splatters of spray on deck.
You knew this long before you saw
the two gods' sheltered harbor cave,
the little man-god's fishy legs,
his trident, and beseeching eyes
turned up to watch the goddess spin her wheel.
Shall he strike the ship and sink it with his goad?
Or part the waves before its struggling prow?
Fortune plies her wheel in fickle time:
Once, Ovid boasted his verse best-loved,
and now, exiled, his books are banned.
A year ago he rode triumphal floats
and now his ship beaches on barbarous sands.

3 Nemesis

Irony, the thing said twice at once,
the bitter side of metaphor.
And what is more ironic than
Nemesis, those sober twins,
each holding in her hand a rod
by which they gauge our evil and our good.
Those opposites that look the same,
always in cahoots with Fate,
they hang around like whores when things go bad,
then, at the end, enter with grave airs,

and tap their palms with their pedantic sticks,
measuring our lives "too little."
The good we tried, they count as wrong.
Amores won for Ovid exile and fame,
and now, in poetry, he curses poems.
The act which made him strong, now makes him lame.
As a boy your father had you study law;
was outraged when he learned you spent your time
on verse. You swore that you would change,
but, helpless, spoke your words in rhyme.

4 Glycon

Head of a lion, muzzle of a sheep,
ear of a woman, eye of an owl,
its long form coils in serpent scales.
Fantastic thing that makes no sense
yet compels us with its power.
Long before the Greeks came here,
and Caesar's greedy legions followed,
Glycon was deity of these shores.
Poet, pray to Glycon's transport, not
the frog-faced monarch who squats in Rome.
Ovid, aging and weak, among barbarians,
forced to arms to defend the walls,
shocked by the horror of a frozen sea,
by "wine in broken chunks of ice,"
"the Getæ's hair tinkling with ice,"
your turning phrase transforms your Fate;
the poem, your metamorphosis.
Not gasping flounder washed ashore,
but mollusk safe on the Seagod's trident.
No poet ever had a home, but the one his art invented.

"THE SMELL OF AUTUMN RAIN..."

The smell of autumn rain and hay hung
about the village, soaking the lungs.
Girls dawdled on the dirty streets
which filled with silence each evening.
The postman shuffled by, slow, hooded, deaf.
Hay wagons – chased by the rain – had left
and silence settled and grew moldy
as simple folk talked at home about Jews.
The drizzle snuffed a gaslight with a hiss,
hissed back by geese waddling to a house.
Leaves were rotting in the old bell's mouth.
We heard these awkward autumn sounds:
the mailcoach rattling in from Dorohoi,
the oxen rising from the bare soil,
bellowing, heads back as if to suck the sky.
The village bellowed back with reddish eyes.

from the Romanian of Benjamin Fundoianu, who died at Auschwitz

THE SIEGE

But when they went out of the city to surrender
they found the enemy nowhere to be seen.
  – Polybius

The city at spearpoint. The army unseen.
Wells stopped, and smoke rising.
Our eagle standard, alive but not with valor,
we ate, without it sticking in our throats.
Then, the plagues. Ghosts from times past,
more faithful to their hearths than we, shot
arrows from ramparts, from far across the fields.
Nothing. Only a star-wound in a god's flesh.
Later, the clock of betrayal struck. Our drawbridge
fell from its pulleys. Cowards, faces to the earth,
begged forgiveness. But no one heard, only the moon
crossing the moat like the bow of a ship on the wind.
Yes, no one. Until the last of our deaths
we shall weep blood and suffer strangely,
doors open to evils, windows shattered.
Not a soul outside the city. But we, we surrendered.

  from the Romanian of Stefan Augustin Doinas

ALL SOULS NIGHT

History records that Pharaoh built the pyramids and that the Emperor
of China built the Great Wall. All by themselves?
  — Bertolt Brecht

It is November. Where the cold hills
fold bleakly into one another
the wind rakes across the slopes
scrubbing last leaves from the trees.
It is November and evening.
A wind is walking dry leaves
up a hillside in chattering ranks
while another gust dashes them down.
November, and the Evening of the Dead.
The moon sails through thin clouds
and villages tucked into alpine valleys
where candles gutter upon the graves
as we wish all souls their rest.

The curled leaves of oak and elm
which skitter across the gravemounds
cannot outnumber the dead,
the rubbish, which Spengler said,
fills up the "trashheaps of history."
For this is the land where peasants
were marched and scattered like leaves,
a land that, often — after Metternich,
the chef d'hôte — the lords of Europe
would carve up like a Christmas goose,
where the Empress Maria Theresa sent
her Schwabisch serfs to plow and sow,
raising meat, bread, blood, and bones
for her armies. Where my grandparents
worked a land that was not theirs.

Both lie buried under iron crosses.
Hers is here below a cedar bough
outside the town at the end of a lane
of poplars, wedded in even pairs.
In the cross's center, under fogged glass,
a photo of her seated with folded arms,
shawl over head, my aunt at her side.
His cross, hammered by my father's hands,
is lost in the stones of the immigrant poor
in Philadelphia, where he died in 1930.
Once, at the steel mill where he worked
he met a man just come from his village.
"The oaks," he asked, "the three oaks
as you enter town. Are they still there?"

Vergil said the dead like blood,
but, really, they are sick of blood,
and hunger most for poetry
which comforts them like well-said mass.
So this is my work this evening
in November, in the dark of All Souls' Night:
Old lady, take this bunch of marigolds;
the aphids are thick on the fuzzy stalks.
How much stronger the plants might have been
if only someone had tended them.
Sleep, and never mind the slug,
its moist side glistening in the candlelight,
as it slides over your hard, dry grave.

Old man, locked in the purgatory of your room,
lit by a bulb that won't shut off
but burns on camp-cot, walnut dresser,
on the peeling wall with Georgian calendar
offering a saint for every day, glaring
in the mirror with frosted edges, always

empty, even when you stand before it,
let me draw you through that mirror now
and place you here beside your wife,
before a grandson you never saw,
who stands here talking to the dead,
to leaves, and wind, and watchful moon.

INSCRIPTIONS FROM THE BLACK SEA TOMBS

I HAIL, WAYFARER. HAVE YOU STOPPED TO WONDER
WHO LIES BURIED HERE? I ENTERED THIS WORLD
IN HELLAS. MY MOTHER CAME FROM ATHENAEN.
MY FATHER FROM HERMIONE. I AM EPIPHANIA.
WITH UNSTAINED HANDS I PLACED MY FATHER
AND MY HUSBAND IN THEIR TOMBS. BOTH SAILORS.
HERMOGENES OF TOMIS, OF THE OINOPE TRIBE,
HAS RAISED THIS IN MY MEMORY.

II YOU SEE HERE THE STONE FIGURE OF CYRIL,
SON OF BESSOS, WHO HAS PASSED IN THE MIDST
OF THE DEAD. HE LOOKED LIKE THIS. TALL.
WHEN HIS COURSE WAS RUN HE WAS BURIED HERE.
HIS LOSS ROUSED GREAT SORROW IN OUR HEARTS.
LONG MAY YOU LIVE, PASSERBY.

III ANDRYS HAS RAISED THIS ROUND FAMILY TOMB
FOR HIS LATE WIFE, KYRILLA, A WOMAN
OF MAIDENLY VIRTUE. THIS GRAVE
FULFILLS AN ETERNAL DUTY.

IV MY NAME WAS HERMOGENES BUT THEY CALLED ME
ALGO THE CYZICIAN. I WAS ARHONTOS IN MY
NATIVE COUNTRY AND I SERVED AS AGORANOMOS
IN ISTRIA. I WAS FRIEND OF NASO, THE POET,
WHO WAS RELEGATUS AND WHO WROTE OF LOVE.
I BROUGHT HIM WINE TO EASE HIS SORROW
AND OIL TO WARM AND RUB HIS AGING FLESH.
HE WROTE FOR ME A POEM IN THE LATIN TONGUE
THAT I MIGHT NEVER DIE. PRAISE THE POET
WHOSE WORDS CAN SAVE AND RAISE THE DEAD.

POETRY READING AT THE VARNA RUINS

The wind skips in from the sea
stirring poplar catkins, wooly stuff
drifting the town in flurries,
nestling like words, like poems,
as we sit in these ancient baths, listening
to poetry, the delicate thing which lasts.
Look at these ruins. Boys, silly with love,
chatted idly by the pools. Merchants,
trading amphoræ of oil and Lydian dye,
muttered about profits, seas, lost ships.
Now seagulls flap and squawk
on broken walls scurfed with weeds,
with weeds and the royal poppy.
Thracian, Greek, Roman, Bulgar, Slav,
Goths, Avars, Celts, Tatars, Huns.
Only poetry lasts.
The walls crumble; Horace endures.
And Ovid saves himself from exile
where history blows off the sea
scattering catkins through rubble of empires.

DR. ALICE MAGHERU'S ROOM

What a mess. The walls cluttered with paintings,
sketches, portraits. Photos: your father-in-law,
Prince Ghica of Samos, and his wife Alexandrina
who played piano with Liszt and Clara Schumann.
Carmen Silva, at her desk, pen in hand. A poem
she wrote for you in feathery blue ink.
The royal family posed beside a car.
A note from Queen Helene that calls you "dear."
Enescu and his nephew walking to a train.
A lithograph of General Magheru, mutton-chopped

hero of the Turkish war, staring resolutely
across the Black Sea, hand on his sword hilt.
And books. Everywhere. Eight thousand books
piled on the floor, crammed into shelves, sliding
off desk tops. Your husband's books of poetry,
his "antipoems" which had more vogue in France
and – leatherbound, titled in thin gold Roman type –
the medical texts you published together.
Bacteriologist, serologist, immunologist,
you made pills as the British bombed Bucharest.

Each night you nap like a cat and read
while others sleep, stretching your eighty-seven
years into twice their human span. Last night
you spoke with your husband, dead for twenty years.
Today, you banter with a poet from America
whose taxi, when he leaves, rattles tram tracks
and cobblestones, halts at a light,
then nudges through crowds on Magheru Boulevard.
Earthquakes and armies have rolled down this street.
You've seen them come and go.

Like sound, the human spirit never dies
but fades, falters, filters off through space,
or is trapped in the laths of marble hearts.
In the quarries of the Parthenon
the shouts of masons murmur still,
caught in crystals like the quartz radio
I played with as a child. So it is, Alice,
with a soul sent out to others, signaling
from this room, this cell of powerful repose,
over the long years: the conscious mind.

COLLATERAL DAMAGE

for Miss Tin in Hue

"The girl (captured; later, freed)
and I (collapsed by a snip of lead)
remember well the tea you steeped
for us in the garden, as music played
and the moon plied the harvest dusk.
You read the poem on a Chinese vase
that stood outside your father's room,
where he dozed in a mandarin dream
of King Gia Long's reposing at Ben Ngu.
We worry that you all are safe.
A house with pillars carved in poems
is floored with green rice fields
and roofed by all the heavens of this world."

...Well, that was the poem, written
in fullest discovery and iambics
by a twenty-four-year-old feeling lucky
not long after those scary events.
Three years later, he (i.e., yours truly)
went back with his young American wife
(not the girl above "captured...freed," etc.)
and the night before the '72 Spring Offensive
(which, you'll recall, almost took the city)
tried to find Miss Tin's house once again
...in a thunderstorm, both wearing ponchos,
and he (a version of "me") clutching a .45 Colt
while she, just clutched his wet hand. Of course,
anyone might have shot us – the Viet Cong
infiltrating the city, the last Marines,
the jittery ARVN troops, or, really,

any wretch just trying to feed his family.
So here's the point: *why would anyone*
(esp. a: me, or b: my wife, or versions of same)
even *dream* of going out like that? ...Simple:
A. To show his bride a household built on poems.
B. To follow love on all his lunkhead ventures.
Anyway, when we found the gated compound,
we scared the wits out of the Vietnamese inside
on the veranda reading by tiny kerosene lamps
or snoozing in hammocks under mosquito netting
who took us for assassins, or ghosts, until
my wife pulled off her poncho hood, revealing
the completely unexpected: a pretty. blond. White Devil.
Since Miss Tin wasn't there, they did the right thing
and denied knowing her, as night and river
hissed with rain and a lone goose honked forlornly.

The next night, we headed out again,
the monsoon flooding the darkened city,
the offensive booming in nearby hills,
and Montagnards trekking into Hue in single file
as their jungle hamlets fell to the barrage.
I kept our jeep running, as my wife dashed out
to give away our piasters to the poor
bastards half-naked in the driving rain.
She gave it all away. Six months' salary,
a sack of banknotes watermarked with dragons,
(except what we needed to get back to Saigon,
but that's another story)...the point here being:
I often think of Miss Tin's pillared house in Hue
and those events now twenty years ago
whenever leaders cheer the new world order,
or generals regret "collateral damage."

MR. GIAI'S POEM

The French ships shelled Haiphong then took the port.
Mr. Giai was running down a road, mobilized
with two friends, looking for their unit in towns
where thatch and geese lay shattered on the roads
and smoke looped up from cratered yards. A swarm
of bullock carts and bicycles streamed against them
as trousered women strained with children, chickens,
charcoal, and rice towards Hanoi in the barrage lull.
Then, Giai said, they saw just stragglers.
Ahead, the horizon thumped with bombs.

At an empty inn they tried their luck
though the waiter said he'd nothing left.
"Just a coffee," said Mr. Giai. "A sip
of whisky," said one friend. "A cigarette," the other.
Miraculously, these each appeared. Serene,
they sat a while, then went to fight.
Giai wrote a poem about that pause for *Ve Quoc Quan*,
the Army paper. Critics found the piece bourgeois.

Forty years of combat now behind him
– Japanese, Americans, and French.
Wounded twice, deployed in jungles for nine years,
his son just killed in Cambodia,
Giai tells this tale to three Americans
each young enough to be his son:
an ex-Marine once rocketed in Hue,
an Army grunt, mortared at Bong Son,
a c.o. hit by a stray of shrapnel,

all four now silent in the floating restaurant
rocking on moor-lines in the Saigon river.
Crabshells and beer bottles litter their table.
A rat runs a rafter overhead. A wave slaps by.
"That moment," Giai adds, "was a little like now."
They raise their glasses to the river's amber light,
all four as quiet as if carved in ivory.

DOGS, DREAMS, AND RAIN

His old mutt stretches out and snores
with oblivion that resembles grace
as cold rains batter the beach house
where he lies awake listening to rain
running off the eaves, rattling the gutter,
as the warm Atlantic thrashes the seawall.

The dog is unburdened by a past,
untroubled by memories; futureless,
harbors no anxious heart.
Oh, every now and then a rabbit
will zigzag through its dreams
and the dog shakes with sleepy yelps,
works its legs, and blinks awake.

Before lying down, it circles its tail,
matting down grass on a Pleistocene plain,
snuffling asleep under a glacial moon.
Dogs huddled for millennia under pelting rain
before human hands took them in.
Who will shelter us caught in thunder
as storms sweep in from the past?

In his rented house in the Florida Keys
he remembers a night below Precious Mountain
before he was domesticated like this dog:
rain slapping the rubbery leaves
of banana trees beside a canal,
geese from the abandoned village
slipping about the muddy bank
near the canal kicking up with rain.

One was honking forlornly, stabbing the air
with cracked blasts like a tenor sax.
A bad set-up, even for a goose, not to mention
him, running a detail on a peculiar mountain
which he couldn't even see through the squalls.

He headed out alone below the palms
bits of things flying in the storm
as the monsoon thrashed the treeline.
He sloshed around all day and never drew fire.
Who says the vc were ever up there? Maybe.
He sighted a lone mule packing opium
through a bamboo thicket on the south side.
He never figured where it came from.
Never found the enemy.
                              So he called in airstrikes,
radioed a chopper, and waited for his ride,
spooked all night as he dozed in the downpour
sunk in his poncho…spooked by geese
and a gibbon screaming in a cave.

Even in the oddest realms – of fear, sleep,
preposterous hopes, drugs, or maybe even dying,
when thoughts skip in the skewed mind like tracers –
a self emerges like a wary hound
trotting out from a flooded banana grove
to sniff the storm and then retreat.
Even as the mind slumbers, and tires
of holding its shape and thoughts
– maps lost, radio dead, poncho leaking –
we are stalked by selves
skirting the shadows like dogs run wild
in elephant grass hissing with rain.

Later on, he saw in *Stars and Stripes* that
The First Air Cavalry swept the mountain.
Whole regiment listed as Missing in Action.

THE CHESS PLAYER

Once our village master at Asian chess,
now you play it Western style.
Rooks and knights and pawns all look the same,
yet you lose at every try.
Somehow the bishop is not a bishop,
and the king over there by the queen
calls up rules you should remember
and rules you should forget
on this odd board of strange moves.
So you lose but keep on playing
at Vietnamese and Western chess
while a yellow butterfly in the garden
flaps about in unpredictable paths.

*translated (with Le Van Canh) from the Vietnamese
of Phan Tien Duat*

READING THE NEWS AND THINKING
OF THE T'ANG POETS

When Li Po tried to climb T'ai-hang,
he found its passes choked with snow.
Thwarted, he turned back to lowlands,
to streams sliding through bare willows
where he sat and fished and wrote a poem.
When young, he was a *hsia* avenger,
righting wrongs with a spoon-headed sword.
Old, he settled things by sitting still.

*

Before the rebels took Ch'ang-an,
Tu Fu escaped the fabled city
where Christian, Jew, and Manichaean
held court with Buddhists. The Emperor,
who wrote lyrics and composed, had fled.
Months later, crossing moonlit fields
stippled bright with human bones,
Tu Fu wrote that poetry is useless,
in a poem alive these thousand years.

*

Today our news is much the same.
Near Srebrenica, skulls dot fields
like cabbages, while in Rwanda,
the short tribe hacked up the tall.
"Blood is smeared on bush and grass,"
yet poetry persists through slaughter,
as if the systoles in our raging hearts
held rhythms that could heal, if heard.

ATOMIC GHOST

As our plane droned south to Peoria
all the cattle ponds and creeks below
caught sun, flared bright, then faded
back into smog seeping from Chicago,
so that looking west through oval ports
you saw jags of water wink and flash.

Then the sky ballooned with light so bright
the firmament bucked and our plane
dropped like a long sigh through magnetized air
and the woman who ordered a Bloody Mary
swirled in her seat, a small cyclone of ash
saying syllables of smoke in the whirligig fire.

Almost at once, cells quirked and recombined.
In the company of scorched ant and armadillo
new lives shuffled forth, sick in their seed,
irradiated, wracked with lunatic genes.
Queer things issued from monsters of the past
as earth reassessed the error that was man,
that was me, my wife, our child. All
entered the pall of incinerated air.

Oh, to be cast from the Garden again and forever.

SOUTH OF L.A.

Wet-suited surfers scud the green combers
and the freeway whines like a wire
here at San Onofre where reactor domes
hump up between sandcliffs and sea
and youngsters promenade the beach
in permed hair and sleekest tans
hoping like hell, for hell is just that:
not to be cast away, to be loved.

As egrets stalk the fouled lagoon
a coot clacks its beak in dry reeds
and, overhead, Camp Pendleton choppers,
Hueys and sleek Cobra gunships,
sweep dragonfly wings in churns of light.

I guess we know this all might blow,
that marsh and egrets, crabs and coots,
tanned teenagers and shimmering shoreline
could be no more than mulch and ash,
atomic smog just drifting out to sea,
drifting past the distant fog bank,
filtering down to the mid-Pacific ridge
that cooks up life in volcanic vents – that
someday our cells may chug through those shafts.

ESTUARY

They walked the footpath to the bay
where waves rinsed the pebbled shore
sloshing cedar roots and sedgy weeds.
Took off their shoes to wade
ankle-deep in cold salt water.
Minnows winked across their toes.
The woman tucked her skirt above her knees
and he slung his coat across his back
as they wandered along without talking
as, farther out, gulls rocked on the tide.
They searched the water slowly
as if it were their hearts and now
and then they bent to lift a stone or shell,
showing them to each other, smiling
as though each had found some wondrous thing.
He found a stone as coral as her lips
and then two tiny spiraled shells, white
and whorled in long perfect turrets.
You never find them whole, he said
and here were two so close together.

TOMATO PICKERS

In the summer, when the sun baked the blacktop
until the tar slid out of it, when the sun
split the ripest tomatoes swelling in the field,
lolling on our shaded porches or shooting slingshots
as we perched in the crotches of mulberry trees,
we'd spot the caravan of old school buses slow up,
saunter off to the dusty shoulder, and stop.
All of the kids would shout "pickers"
and we'd head out through the chest-high weeds
swatting down the heavy cups of Queen Anne's lace
with willow switches, ten or so of us;
who would dare each other to the edge
of the green sunny field already moving with
black-skinned men and women, bending over
fat tomatoes rowed in the dusty earth.
Someone said they carried knives on their backs.
I couldn't see how. One of us shouted "Niggers!"
We ran. The kerchiefed women hardly turned.

Later, after a rain, I'd go out in the field
looking for flint arrowheads and box turtles.
I'd see the pickers' footprints, bare and shod,
still planted in the earth, some trod tomatoes
with bright pulpy seeds, a few lunch-wrappers.

Once when I was old enough to hunt with my father,
we crossed the frosted field, then planted in turnips,
to get to a briar patch. As my father bent down
to root out a turnip, I remembered that an old black woman
had been found dead in a thicket near the field.
Wandered off and died. Kids found her.

My father pared off the purply dark skin; cut a slice.
The white sliver I chewed made me feel odd.

SOME NOTES ON MIAMI

SNAILS

slide across the air-conditioned glass
as morning sun plunges through our windows.
Poor disoriented mollusks, gliding nowhere but easily
in *glissando* waltz through beads of condensation
stretching out their knobby eyes for the aubade's edge,
for stone's shade below *las flores*, in Florida.

*

PARROTS

With half the trees derived from Africa or Asia
perhaps even parrots will replace the native birds
or so this pair of cracker doves, perched on a wire,
seem to nod to one another,
as parrots thrash the mango leaves
shrieking tree to tree.

Parrot, lorikeet, roller, toucan – all
loosed from cages and free in Miami –
assault the air with raucous squawks,
calling up flocks for their new world order.

*

ALLIGATOR

How could any creature that might spend eternity
as pocketbook or pair of shoes, or simply
trapped in a sinkhole, take the risk?
Rising off the mucky bottom, roiling the river,

plated brow specked with duckweed, jaws
lunging up, clamping on the child's head
dragging him under, as his father
bashed the water with an oar, how?
After dissection, the vet said
it looked hungry. El Lagarto: the lizard.

*

Hurricane

Naked, floating face down in the TV room
now filled with seawater seeping from glass doors
he had duct-taped against the hurricane,
the room a dark aquarium, his white body, bobbing
– he must have been asleep on the couch, exhausted
after a day of battening down the house
when baysurge beached in a swarm of seaspouts
churning up the mangrove swamp, the great wave colliding,
breaching doors, collapsing walls, wallowing, then
tumbling back out as winds shrieked off treetops,
sea slosh sucking up drowned frogs, broken snakes,
skinned pelicans, dragging leaf muck, sparkles of
shattered glass, lawn chairs, rolling a dead manatee,
slopping back through tangles of trees, impaled boats,
to the seesaw bay sizzling with rain, leaving him
rocking in a kelp of curtains, arms outstretched
toward something in the green cloudy water.

*

The Cuban Rafter

At the dock behind his house in Islamorada
he cranks the windlass and lifts his boat from the bay.
Below, lobsters tickle antennæ at murky pilings
while the ibis paces the jetty, anxious
for any prawns brought back in the bucket,
for wrasse and yellowtails languid in their pails.

But now, bare-backed, bending to the weight on the winch,
ignoring the frantic bird, the freckled man pulls up his boat,
the scar across his shoulder just a purply burl
in the rose light of evening.
                         Boat secured,
he studies the reef where his raft had drifted
into... *the snorkeling school from the Cheeca Lodge,*
the drivers' eyes big, big behind their masks,
all waving to come see him, burnt-faced, silent,
lying on a wooden raft, alone upon the waves...
"Hola, primo," he says to the manatee rising by the dock
like a luminous submarine, "Hola," he says,
and reaches in a hamper for heads of lettuce saved
for this prop-scarred blimp that begs its dinners
from wealthy docks along the Key,
from him, now the "guayabera shirt-king of Miami"
whose raft was waterless on the sixth day out
who landed here without his wife
her last words whimpered through blistered lips
before she rolled off under a Bahamian swell,
whose first job was janitor at the Biltmore
whose melanoma almost ate his socket out
who made six million dollars in eighteen years
who now has a family and house in Hialeah
and who comes here alone when he can on weekends

to chase kingfish and snook, to listen to wavewash
to toss baits to the loony bird haunting his dock
to drop a hose to the manatee thirsty for fresh water,
whom he calls his "cousin" and tells to drink.

＊

Etymologies of the Post-Colonial Iguana

*Gwanes they have, which is a little harmlesse beast, like a Crokadell or
Alligator, very fat and good meat.*
  – Capt. John Smith, 1630

Iwana [<Carib>], Iuannas, Wanaes, Gwanes, Iguana.
There's the common green iguana from Columbia
which eats hibiscus and bananas
and its cousin, *iguana delicatissima,*
which indicates the problem for this harmless beast:

gallina del palo, they call it in Spanish
in *las Americas* and throughout the Caribbean:
"chicken of the tree."
                    Mr. Dieu-Donné Telforêt,
Monsieur "Given-by-God from the Distant Forest,"
my Haitian cabbie who takes me into town,
keeps his iguana in a halter on the passenger seat,
whether as dinner or *amie* I can't say.

＊

Saturday Night

At Bayside, a crowd enjoys an outdoor concert
as lasers shoot green streaks across the sky.
On South Beach the kids parade in silly clothing.
In Hialeah, there's a meeting of Alpha 66. Somewhere
the *santería* are cutting throats of chickens.
Everywhere the rich are showing off their wealth.
While at a darkened Wal-Mart where the Everglades begin
inside the Garden Shop, at wilderness's edge,
green-glow *cucuyo* fireflies light rows of oleander
and a swamp-rattler curls inside a potted palm.

*

Red Dust

Rising off the droughts of Africa, the dry pans
of the Atlas mountains, the Sahara, the El Djouf,
swirling up from parched fields, the rich dust
sails on stratospheric winds across the Atlantic,
sifts down onto the Amazon, rains upon the Everglades,
falling here this Sunday morning, in Miami
where we brush it from our cars, perplexed.

ANNA AKHMATOVA SPENDS THE NIGHT ON MIAMI BEACH

Well, her book, anyway. The Kunitz volume
left lying on a bench, the pages
a bit puffy by morning, flushed with dew,
riffled by sea breeze, scratchy with sand
– the paperback with the 1930s photo
showing her in spangled caftan, its back cover
calling her "star of the St. Petersburg circle
of Pasternak, Mandelstam, and Blok,
surviving the Revolution and two World Wars."

So she'd been through worse...
the months outside Lefortovo prison
waiting for a son who was already dead, watching
women stagger and reel with news of executions,
one mother asking, "Can you write about this?"
Akhmatova thought, then answered, "Yes."

If music lured her off the sandy bench
to the clubs where men were kissing
that wouldn't have bothered her much
nor the vamps sashaying in leather.
Decadence amid art deco fit nicely
with her black dress, chopped hair, Chanel cap.
What killed her was the talk, the empty eyes,
which made her long for the one person in ten thousand
who could say her name in Russian,
who could take her home, giving her a place
between Auden and Apollinaire
to whom she could describe her night's excursion
amid the loud hilarities, the trivial hungers
at the end of the American century.

SORT OF A GAY-BASH

Remember, I was barely twenty-one.
All through college I had lived off loans
and itty-bitty scholarships, working summers.
That day I won a big-time fellowship:
My first free summer lay ahead,
first free year. I mention this
as background, not excuse. That night,

bombed and happy, I looked for friends
among the bars on College Avenue,
found Art and Roger in the My-O-My
sitting with some older, beefy guy
in business suit and feathered hat
who said, as I settled in the booth,
"A shame the people they let in here."

It's true I stank of booze, but Jesus.
Who *was* this bozo, anyway? Annoyed,
adrift inside my drunken funk,
I ordered boilermakers, watched them talk.
I wanted to explain my day's good luck,
buy them drinks, talk about my plans. Instead,
this overstuffed *suit* with an attitude.

"Let me guess," I said, "Salesman, maybe.
Maybe FBI. *Maybe* just a pansy on the prowl."
He said "say that again" he'd punch me.
So I said it all again and jumped
as the punch came, cracking my ribs and not
my jaw but knocking me out of the booth
onto the beer-splashed, greasy floor.

Furious, and meaner now than any skunk,
I wobbled up, brushed off the peanut shells,
and slammed a fist below his nose
collapsing Mr. Tons-of-Fun to frat-rat cheers
as bouncers rushed to throw us out
hauling us upstairs and out the door
to a mayblossom street hushed by rain.

Where things got *really* strange as the guy
kept coming at me with such crazy swings
I suckerpunched him, ear, stomach, face
and left him kneeling on the sidewalk, blood
dribbling off his nose and down his suit.
My friends walked me home, oddly silent.
"Weird," Art said, "he only hit you once."

A few weeks later, there he was again:
marching in the Memorial Day Parade
with the lederhosened Little German Band,
puckering a tuba, fat cheeks puffing,
his chubby knees marking time, innocent
as oom-pah-pah despite his public beating
and me, confused with all of this. Ashamed.

FOR JOHN HAAG, LOGGER, SAILOR, HOUSEPAINTER, POET, PROFESSOR, AND GROWER OF ORCHIDS

"Pass in, pass in," the angels say…
"by the stairway of surprise."
  — Emerson, "Merlin I"

This is between you and me, Haag.
In this College of Glooms
you saunter about in leather pants
pacing the halls as if they were a deck
from your sailing days in the Merchant Marine

…as if you were here on shore leave
and had to make ship in Seattle
tonight…tailing trucks through snowy foothills
as flurries veer at your windshield
and brake lights blink ahead on the turns
as you chant to yourself and the snow
all the poems you ever learned alone
on moon-washed nights when waves were listening:
Dylan Thomas. Wallace Stevens.
"The Ashtabula Bridge Disaster."
…yes, squinting into the dark and saying poems,
passing a truck on the straightaway
driving hard until you hit Puget Sound
where the sea rushed the rocks on the beach
under a fat moon wreathed in fog
and the bell buoy chimes all night.

This is between the two of us, not
those who speculate, but never make;
who lodge in our mansion in rented rooms

and have tacked old carpets down
over all the holes in the floors. They
shall never mount the stairway of surprise
which angels showed us
unless we are their guides
up to the belfry where the sea is crashing
and the bell rings waves of light.

VIEWING THE NEW WORLD ORDER

Each structure, in its beauty, was even then and at once antique,
but in the freshness of its vigor, even today, recent and newly wrought.
   – Plutarch, on the Acropolis

In old-town Athens of date palms, of ferned balconies
cascading canary calls, I walk with a Bulgarian friend
up the stony sunshine path to the "high city" where
tangles of cactus and spanish sword pock the Periclean ramparts
and packs of wild cats prowl the brush for mice as a wind
whips the naps of their fur and Georgi's little son, Aleko,
hoots after them as we trail behind, plodding upward
through the gate of broken columns to the precincts of Athena,
two poets, from West and East, here for the first time, awed
by the lonely grace of stones fallen, stones still standing.

        *

On the left, the smiling maidens of the karyatid porch
whose marble robes flutter in blue sky;
on the right, the massive surge of Parthenon columns
capped by a parade of centaurs, horsemen, gods,
reliving dramas of who we are, who we might become
as pediments mark our battles with beasts, our talks
with gods, our search for ourselves in philosopher groves
of this city on the hill that draws us by surviving
Persian navies, Roman consuls, pasha's yoke, and *Panzer Gruppe,*
holding up like a Phidean model a sense
of the examined life that is worth living, a place
where gods and men could struggle with success, striving
to widen the wealth of the human soul, the size of heaven.
All across the monumental rubble, trailing after tour guides,
Japanese photograph this field of broken stone.

*

This is the New World Order my President would praise:
both superpowers more or less broke; the Japanese our bankers.
Looking east from the Acropolis, past Yugoslavian slaughter,
the Kozlodui reactor's about to blow.
Further on, in Tbilisi, the shoot-out at Parliament,
the breadlines in Moscow, the dead rivers and lakes,
the black colonels hopping in Rumpelstiltskin rage
at loss of empire, as Chechens, Kurds, Azeris et al.
go for their guns to settle old scores.

*

This is the realm of Israeli rubber bullet and Arab stone.
Of holiday shoppers at Clapham Junction bombed by Irish
     Santas.
German skinheads bashing Vietnamese and Turks.
Of bloated African bellies, of fly-infested eyes.
Of Shining Path Maoists beheading Indians in Ayacucho.
As nosferatu warlords in Beijing sip their elixir
of cinnabar and blood. And Pol Pot vacations in Thailand.

*

It's snowing in Chicago, snowing on the cardboard huts
of homeless in the land of the free, as more banks fail
and repossessed Midwestern farms lie fallow to the wind.
When the Wall fell to hurrahs of freed multitudes
one could hear communist gasps and capitalist sighs rise up
in global shout which circled the earth for a year
then disappeared through holes in the ozone layer.

*

The new world order. The tribes of the Book
are still turned to wrath as the worst of us
would wind time back to savage pasts easier to imagine.
The philosopher's grove is empty; the poet's words gone flat.
Against this, aren't the Japanese, baptized in nuclear fire,
clapping their hands for the Kami of the cash register,
our safest, sanest neighbors?

*

        These old stones cry out for more.
Surviving centuries, sculpted here for all to see,
the handsome youth, the maiden at the well, their inward smiles,
declare our need for beauty and laws like love
for this tiny *polis* of a planet spinning wildly,
for my daughter, snug, now asleep in her bed,
for Aleko who played in the Chernobyl cloud,
whose father now stands near the Nike's rotting frieze,
looking out upon the city jammed with cars. Georgi
opens his flask of vodka and pours some on a stone
before we drink our toasts to the new world order,
to cedars shrill with locusts in the heat of summer,
to whatever muse shall come to give us words.

LOCUST GHAZAL-DAZZLE

While summer lingered late in trees,
locusts tried to orchestrate the trees

in shrill cantatas tumbling through the shade
upon a boy alone and staring up at trees.

Alone with himself, listening for a voice,
he heard the whine of insect wings in trees

buried long and mute beneath the ground
but rising now in branch tops through the trees,

a canopy of song between dark earth and sky,
spilling sunlight and kindred calls in trees.